SOCIAL INTELLIGENCE IN EVERYDAY LIFE

I0414072

C. Margaret Hall

Social Intelligence in Everyday Life *is a guide to discovering the power and complexity of social influences, and the impact they have on our freedom and opportunities. This book is dedicated to readers who want to better themselves and the world we live in.*

Table of Contents

Sources of Social Intelligence

Understanding
Social Intelligence

I. What is Social Intelligence?

The first section of *Social Intelligence in Everyday Life*, "Understanding Social Intelligence," presents different ways to define and explain social intelligence (sometimes referred to as "SI"). Definitions of social intelligence are followed by explorations of how social intelligence is learned, what social intelligence does for us, and the risks and hazards we expose ourselves to when we do not deliberately try to build this resource. Some of these approaches are described in this introductory chapter.

Social intelligence is knowledge about the complexities of social dependencies and patterns of interaction in society. Social intelligence derives from a deep understanding of self in society, a broad perspective on how societies change or perpetuate themselves, and an awareness of the inextricable connections among self, society, and the global community.

Social intelligence is acquired automatically, and at deep emotional levels during the earliest stages of childhood. It can be more deliberately cultivated in adult years. SI is a valuable form of life-long learning that becomes a resource and a reliable guide in all kinds of decision-making and behavior. Different levels of social intelligence are found in individuals, groups, societies, and the international community.

Like anything else that has a powerful influence over us, such as science or religion, social intelligence may be used for constructive or destructive purposes. Ideally, when oriented toward increasing the common good, SI changes the course of history for the better, as well as resolves major interpersonal and social problems.

1

Unfortunately, social intelligence is also an objective and accessible resource that may be used to strategize genocide and other social atrocities. However, such potential for evil-doing through social intelligence is ignored in *Social Intelligence in Everyday Life*. This book places an exclusive emphasis on the life-enhancing, beneficial consequences of increasing social intelligence.

One of the most interesting facts about social intelligence is that there is a direct connection between knowledge of society and self-knowledge. At the same time that we get to know more about society, we discover more about ourselves. One development of this link is that social knowledge empowers the self and leads toward more effective redesigns of both self and society.

Society is reflected within us and in our reactions to society. There is no escape from experiencing some deep-seated social influences on our behavior, even though we may not be aware of them, or may not acknowledge or understand the extent of their impact. However, we are who we are largely because we have been brought up to acknowledge and respect particular social rules and expectations.

Paying close attention to the events that occur in our lives enables us to learn from them, and to increase our social intelligence. When we set out to size up different social situations, and to achieve objectivity about our identities and our tasks, we learn a great deal about our immediate social conditions, society, and ourselves. Furthermore, if we make a habit of seriously considering what we stand for, and what we want to accomplish in the broadest contexts of our lives, we can make more accurate and effective assessments of our contributions to society.

Because social intelligence is learned, social intelligence is ours for the taking. Social intelligence can be thought of as a personal talent, capacity, or ability that can be exercised, as well as a cultural product. Social intelligence is expressed in individual, interpersonal, and social behavior, and is at the same time an integral part of our culture. For instance, family responsibilities should at best be assumed with social intelligence. Both popular culture and high culture are resources of social intelligence, which suggest ranges of choices about how family responsibilities can be defined.

Even though human beings live in widely varied social and economic circumstances, some specific principles of social

I. What is Social Intelligence?

intelligence can be applied to diverse sets of conditions. Knowledge about human and social dependency is a vital starting point for building SI. We only know ourselves more fully when we consider our personal relationships in the context of more impersonal but familiar social systems. It is because of this significant principle of the power of human dependency that, for example, Islamic communities wield so much influence over their individual members, or that individuals struggle to be autonomous in Western societies.

Social intelligence derives from all forms of social sources, but some contexts have more powerful influences over individuals and groups than others. Some of the most significant social influences in both our formative and adult years are our families, religions, social classes, cultures, and societies. These five institutionalized patterns of interaction leave clear imprints on our being and behavior, whether or not we knowingly accept or conform to these influences. Consequently, we need to come to terms with these strong social anchors in our lives if we are to be free and productive members of society.

The second section of *Social Intelligence in Everyday Life*, "Sources of Social Intelligence," examines the various characteristics of the strong influences of these five patterns of interaction on our behavior. Separate chapters describe and explain why these particular intersections in individuals' complex relationships affect their social intelligence, as well as their roles in accomplishing change. Related significant social influences, such as gender, are also addressed in these chapters.

The third and final section of *Social Intelligence in Everyday Life*, "Future Directions," covers major possibilities for the development, transmission, and application of social intelligence. Because the farthest corners of the world are increasingly accessible through travel and electronic communications, and because we are participants in a single global economy, it is imperative that we use SI to meet ever-increasingly broad collective needs as well as individual goals. We must find effective ways to go beyond both political rhetoric and traditional sources of wisdom if we are to survive and thrive in this new century. However, in spite of our tremendous technological advances, we can only plan effectively when we also pay sufficient attention to what it means to be interdependent human beings. In addition we must learn from errors we have made at all levels of social organization if we are to create a better tomorrow for all.

In order to ensure that we cover such a broad scope of change, the collective "we" must be as inclusive and representative a voice as possible, taking into account the voices of those who are unable to articulate their own interests and needs. When we understand the power of interdependencies both within and between societies, we shall be more able to act effectively on our behalf as well as for others. Thus it is in everyone's interest to make sure that there are no weak links in our chains of interdependency, and that our resources are distributed in ways that eliminate as much suffering as possible while protecting the whole. We gain nothing in the long run from pursuing narrow, selfish goals, and using social intelligence helps us to keep this broader picture clearly in mind.

Dimensions of Social Intelligence

Although analysis can be disadvantageous because it frequently compartmentalizes and fragments important realities, taking a brief look at some of the basic dimensions of social intelligence is helpful. One dimension of SI is the cultivation of a detailed and more direct awareness of who we are. This includes building knowledge about our attitudes toward self and others; our ideals, values, and beliefs; our goals; our habits and behavior; and our inclinations to monitor what we do and what happens to us.

Another dimension of social intelligence expands this personal focus, and examines how we relate to significant others in dyads, triads, families, and kin groups. Our experiences of family dependencies also influence the kinds of religious or educational choices we make, how we define our everyday realities and world views, and how we see ourselves in relation to other crucial groups such as our work systems, peers, or social classes. Our family connections predispose us toward certain patterns of behavior, the social bonds we form, and the social goals we choose to make our own.

Knowing to which social class we belong, or how others place us in specific racial, ethnic, or gender groups, is another significant dimension of social intelligence. Even though economic class membership, for example, may not seem important to us, others'

I. What is Social Intelligence?

attitudes about our economic status can influence us significantly, largely determining how freely we operate in the broader society, and how we make our most important economic decisions.

Other social groups to which we belong, or to which others see us as belonging, may have just as strong an impact on our actions as economic class. For example, being female in a sexist society, or being black in a racist society, strongly influences how we interact with others, and how others relate to us.

Social intelligence also has a cultural dimension. This aspect links us to the dominant values and belief systems of society, so that our education or age group may predispose us to act in certain ways, according to their shared cultural preferences. For example, we are more likely to enjoy a high culture of classical literature and symphony concerts if we are well-educated or adult, and more likely to participate in popular culture if we are less well-educated or adolescent. However, SI frequently counteracts these general patterns. As we learn more about ourselves in society, we can deliberately change our level of cultural participation by deciding to behave differently from other members of our groups.

Another basic strand of social intelligence is the ability to see our life situations more objectively. We increase our social intelligence when we see ourselves and other people with objectivity in considering social interaction in the contexts of our own society, other societies, and the world system. Using SI in this way helps us to recognize our privileges and disadvantages with reference to the totality of our worlds, so that we can act more effectively.

In reality, these separate dimensions of social intelligence function together as a whole. Furthermore, we cannot separate the micro- and macro-dimensions of SI in our social experiences if we are socially intelligent about our participation in our societies. Paradoxically, we are at once microcosms and macrocosms of human agency in society.

Individuals interact within the social structures of families, religions, classes, cultures, and societies; they also participate in creating and sustaining these structures. It is in the reciprocal give and take of everyday life that patterns of behavior settle and become recognizable as social structures, which are inextricably linked to individuals, especially through these specific dimensions of social intelligence. Because individuals are essentially actors in establishing their own characteristic patterns of interaction, they are instrumental in bringing about changes and shifts in these same interactions. Social intelligence, due to its comprehensiveness and its influence on motivation and human agency, is particularly useful for identifying needs, designing strategies for change, and carrying out these changes.

Feeling and Reason

Social intelligence is different from emotional intelligence, and from the more traditional concept of cognitive intelligence, because it is a synthesis of selected aspects of both emotional and cognitive intelligence. Unlike emotional intelligence, which is the ability to manage and express feelings appropriately, and unlike cognitive intelligence, which is the ability to think and to reason, SI expressly strives to balance and integrate an awareness of feelings with the abilities to think and reason. By focusing on both subjective and objective realities, social intelligence consists of knowledge and practical skills based on feedback from feelings, as well as on observations and applications of thought and reason to everyday problem solving.

Social intelligence includes a rational understanding of emotional patterns in social exchanges, of emotional meanings attributed to social behavior, and of the kinds of emotional investments people make in particular socio-cultural goals. In the special case of self-knowledge, SI makes use of individuals' awareness of their emotions and feelings, so that this information becomes a resource and guide for intellectual or cognitive analyses. In these respects, social intelligence goes beyond the focus on appropriate affective expressions characterizing emotional intelligence, to discovering the deepest social sources and the most far-reaching social consequences of emotions and feelings in social life.

Cultures and societies have emotional characteristics and styles as well as individuals. For example, in previous historic times in Western society, it was customary to feel modest about the body, largely due to religious influences, and also to be relatively emotionally detached from one's children, usually because there was a strong possibility that the children would predecease the adults. In addition, in both past and contemporary societies, negative feelings have served as effective social controls,

I. What is Social Intelligence?

especially in family and gender relations, and positive feelings essentially as rewards for conforming to established norms and cultural standards of success and achievement.

Social intelligence is the capacity to see emotions and feelings for what they are, by understanding emotions and feelings in a relatively rational, objective way. SI also acknowledges the importance of emotions in the biology of human relations. Although many important distinctions can be made between biological and social characteristics of human beings, one significant aspect of the human condition is that social emotions can be used to either increase or limit the productivity and effectiveness of individuals and societies.

Because social intelligence must assess the impact of subjective experiences on perceptions, understanding, and behavior, individual and social expressions of emotions and feelings need to be taken seriously at all times. For example, SI makes use of impressions, emotions, and feelings to explore the characteristics and strengths of social influences and motivations. It also analyzes impressions, emotions, and feelings in broad social and historical contexts, which allows subjectivity to be understood more objectively and more fully.

A scrutiny of our everyday exchanges in this kind of holistic perspective shows that stresses in personal relationships often reflect broad trends or conflicts in society, such as those found in gender and family relations. The emotional abuse of women is both an interpersonal interaction and a cultural pattern, enacted and re-enacted in small group milieus in past and present societies. A socially intelligent person sees the vital connections between these microscopic and macroscopic social realities, and seeks to solve emotional abuse problems by changing both aspects of the abusive situations.

Many societies invest strong feelings and emotions in their most cherished traditions, often for no more apparent reason than to continue these same traditions. Because of the strength of collective emotional investments in traditions, it is especially difficult to change social structures and norms in traditional societies, even when plans to bring about changes are based on thought and reason. In contrast to these conservative patterns and tendencies, social intelligence routinely challenges tradition by calling into question the extent to which the interests of all the

7

people in a given society are met by perpetuating that society's traditions. Applying social intelligence to problematic circumstances and conditions is frequently a first step toward making changes to increase the common good, instead of automatically perpetuating the inequitable status quo.

Unfoldment

By necessity, social intelligence changes some of its substantive emphases over time due to the shifting priorities and developing structures of cultures and societies. Because SI is learned, its content is influenced by the transitions society goes through as it adapts to new local, national, and global conditions. The broad scope of concerns encompassed by social intelligence makes it inevitable that history must continue to influence what social intelligence is, for example. At the same time, personal development and the attainment of maturity bring other kinds of everyday influences to bear on the content and meaning of social intelligence.

One basic principle of social intelligence is that individuals' inner states of well-being generally reflect different kinds of external social conditions and their direct responses to broad social changes, especially in times of major political crises such as wars and revolutions. We are inherently social creatures, and consequently, at least in some vital respects, the social products of cultures and societies. We are also historical beings, because the life of our cultures and societies creates relentless motion and change.

In order to be effective strategists in the present and future, we must think of social intelligence as evolving directly from the past. For instance, after two hundred years' experience of the industrial revolution, we have come to understand some of the reasons why industrialization and urbanization can decrease the quality of life in society. In spite of the fact that industrialization has raised the standard of living for many peoples, and in spite of marked increases in the availability and range of material goods produced, crime and alienation have also increased, as have some persisting inequities among social classes, races, genders, and ethnic groups.

Social intelligence necessarily includes this kind of unfolding knowledge about historical changes. This resource helps us to create more enlightened social policies to deal with some of the critically

I. What is Social Intelligence?

negative and unintended consequences of industrialization. Because we have observed and endured many different kinds of dramatic social reorganization during the last two hundred years, we are now able to understand more about complex aspects of change than was possible before this time. Keeping this social knowledge current and connected to appropriate historical contexts helps us to apply social intelligence in making effective plans for the future. A historically informed social intelligence strengthens the outcomes of various policy interventions, and it is because of these connections that we need to consider a broad historical sweep of social realities in resolving difficult social problems.

From a historical perspective, social intelligence can help us to understand the coercive powers of a given social order, as well as its particular kinds of social change. When we examine the many ways in which society remains stable, it is useful to acknowledge the extent of the enmeshment between our identities and various social institutions such as families, religions, the economy, education, and political systems. We have become who we are because of the influence of these basic mechanisms of social survival. Therefore personal stability is necessarily rooted in these foundations and social anchors of society.

During the last two centuries, families have changed their forms and distinctive patterns of interaction because they have had to adapt to the compelling demands of capitalist economies. Families in many industrialized societies have lost their stability and security due to market forces; they have been disconnected from ancestors, elders, and third generation family members. By contrast, less-developed countries tend to offer their families more protections from hazards in the outer world because of their stronger social traditions and complex intergenerational connections. However, members of families in less developed countries may be so oppressed by their responsibilities in meeting their families' needs that they cannot achieve sufficient independence to pursue their own goals. Therefore, from a historical perspective, we can learn much about what it takes for families to function well in terms of their abilities to protect and support their members.

When social institutions such as the family or religion change, they create rifts or social dislocations in broader society. The constant shifts in these basic social realties make it difficult to define social intelligence. However, there is a definable constancy accompanying this quality of the historical specificity of social intelligence. What serves individuals and society best, with respect to accommodating or adapting to social change, or in terms of challenging the status quo, is the flexibility of social intelligence. One of the most persistent and most significant characteristics of SI through time is that it is an open-ended system of knowledge that is continuously being consolidated and reformed.

Reciprocity

A significant consequence of being a social creature is that people predictably react to others' behavior. Because none of us can survive in a vacuum, or in isolation from each other, there is no way to escape from these bonds of reciprocity. Human beings are interdependent, and their relationships are inevitably complex, consisting of overlapping layers of dependency and reactivity.

Social intelligence includes an awareness of the many kinds of connections that individuals and groups forge with each other, the controls that society exerts on its members, and the dynamics of the generally predictable responses that follow in the wake of individual or group actions. Our exchanges with others are based largely on our expectations and predictions of what others will do, and our beliefs in what we think are appropriate responses help to keep society together. Social intelligence includes knowing the extent to which society is organized around this principle of reciprocity, and how individuals can use the principle to maintain stability or precipitate change.

The unavoidable influence of reciprocity on our behavior is often much stronger than people's individual respect for everyday social conventions. For example, the principle of reciprocity draws us into exchanges with others that we may not really want, and we are more tied to those we care for than we realize or find comfortable. Furthermore, it is because of the principle of reciprocity that we tend to repeat many social customs: it is usually much easier to conform than to be different, and people tend to go with the flow, rather than to act independently.

Because it is both challenging and exhausting to go against the tide of social expectations or public opinion, we cannot counter the principle of reciprocity at every turn. Therefore it is frequently more socially intelligent to wait for significant opportunities to express ourselves independently than to indiscriminately try to expend the effort and energy necessary to stand up for our deepest beliefs at all times.

Social intelligence encompasses knowledge of these powerful reciprocal and reactive pressures in everyday life. A socially intelligent person knows how to deal with people in both peaceful and conflicted situations, and how to accomplish tasks independently, in the face of opposition. Social ideals like love, respect, and empathy are effective guides for reciprocal interaction, especially in stressful situations, and social intelligence suggests ways to meet individual and social needs given the ever-present base of reciprocity.

Because of the crucial importance of the complex qualities of reciprocity, we have to work hard to size up the situations in which we find ourselves. Understanding the human condition requires some ability to put ourselves in others' positions, so that we can see where they are coming from and understand their reactions. Only when we really respect and know others, can we meet their needs as well as our own. Furthermore, when people are unable to express their real interests, we have a duty to assist them and to work toward improving the common good for our own benefit as well as for theirs. In fact, we can only continue to be strong if, at the same time, we help others to be strong. Our collective well-being depends on the weakest as well as the strongest links in our chains of dependency.

Reciprocity is thus the intrinsic give and take of social behavior, and social intelligence is a reliable guide to dealing effectively with others' needs as well as our own. One important caveat is that we cannot spend all of our energies attending to others' needs. Social intelligence emphasizes the importance of addressing our own needs first, and of balancing our needs with those of others. SI directs behavior so that we can really make a difference, preventing us from spinning our wheels in impossibly difficult situations. It also helps us to select appropriate goals and behavior amid the strong tides of reciprocity. We are less likely to be trapped or enmeshed in complex reactive patterns of reciprocity when we act with social intelligence.

Resistance

Social intelligence is the ability to question vested interests and assumptions about society and social relationships. It is because of this questioning posture that social intelligence is able to challenge the establishment and the status quo, if only by moving toward exposing hidden patterns of dominance. By doing this, social intelligence predictably precipitates resistance from groups wishing to maintain social conditions as they are.

Because the simplest exercise of social intelligence has the potential to call into question the powers that be, SI is resisted. Even though applying social intelligence increases beneficially innovative or creative contributions, these also may be automatically resisted, at least in the short run.

A socially intelligent person recognizes that this kind of resistance occurs, and garners sufficient personal strength or collective resources to sustain efforts to make proposed changes, thereby overcoming resistance in the long run. In these respects social intelligence serves as an effective discipline to deal with others' reactivity, so that rather than allowing discouragement to set in, more productive strategies are used. For example, a socially intelligent person will choose to make repeated requests, revise or create new documents when needed, find new avenues of expression, organize stronger support from others, or temporarily back down, rather than give up a venture. Renewed efforts to proceed are developed from using socially intelligent strategies.

Therefore, someone with a high level of social intelligence does not withdraw when faced with resistance, but instead continues to advance slowly with more caution and increased ingenuity. Practicing SI means that efforts to accomplish specific goals may have to be expanded and redesigned rather than cut back or withdrawn.

If the substance of social intelligence—or its larger purpose—behind a proposed project can be communicated to those who resist, in addition to the concrete details of the proposal, resistance can gradually become acceptance and even support for the project. Both individual and collective persistence are more likely to be successful when they are guided by social intelligence, rather than driven by sheer determination, or sustained by efforts that are diluted or intimidated by the resistance.

This principle of resistance to innovation can be observed between individuals, groups, nations, or blocs of nations. Stability between two conflicting parties may be achieved by engaging a

I. What is Social Intelligence?

third party to balance the power of the two parties who are at an impasse. However, a resolution of resistance occurs only through a gradually achieved mutual acknowledgment of the benefits of the initially resisted proposal. By contrast, attempts to forcefully impose new social designs on others are predictably resisted with fervor, and may quickly generate severe tensions or combat.

Social intelligence therefore includes knowledge of diplomatic strategies for managing power imbalances, skills to behave constructively in stressful circumstances, and a deep and comprehensive understanding of others' real needs. SI is achieved through close scrutiny of experiences, observations, and reflections, and through learning about patterns in social behavior and social organizations.

Certain strategies of civil disobedience are based on these principles of social intelligence. Civil rights leaders demonstrated a practical application of social knowledge in the face of conflict and tension-ridden resistance, so that gradually more equitable policies were accepted and institutionalized as law. Although much resistance to civil rights remains to be dealt with, one important source for the future success of the civil rights movement is to continue to cultivate social intelligence, and to deliberately apply it to specific proposals and strategies in bringing about these changes.

Another form of resistance to achieving needed changes is a denial of social facts, or a refusal to define and understand problems in their broadest social contexts. For example, a woman who suffers from depression in her home may have a physiological condition that relates more directly to her isolation or to her status in society than to an internal disorder. When she becomes aware of the broader causes of her discomfort, she will be able to start to reduce her own inner resistance to making changes in her life, in turn developing her social intelligence more freely.

Social intelligence sheds light on the problem of finding effective solutions to others' resistance; it is more effective than conventional problem-solving because the general social conditions of a particular situation are kept in focus. SI allows us to see and understand the larger pictures of our lives, so that the most compassionate and constructive contributions can be created, in spite of others' resistance.

Questions

Any description or discussion of the nature of social intelligence quickly becomes problematic because it must involve myriad complex ambiguities and nuances. Explanations and affirmations about social intelligence's nature also precipitate endless questions, some of which are unanswerable. However, questions about social intelligence can be a useful guide to further explorations of SI, because undirected forays into the unknown or difficult-to-define social realities are often unproductive. In fact, the reports and issues about SI in *Social Intelligence in Everyday Life* are shaped more by these kinds of continuing questions than by claims of having definitive answers.

Before looking at some of the most basic questions considered in *Social Intelligence in Everyday Life*, it is important to understand that no questions about SI are too trivial to take seriously or to try to answer, especially because many of the seemingly unimportant aspects of our everyday lives are frequently connected to the foundations of society in some way. It is therefore useful to think of questions, however simple, as being significant leads for exploring the deepest mysteries of life and social relations. Questions are vital means and aids in our immediate task of defining and understanding social intelligence.

In answering the central question of the first chapter of *Social Intelligence in Everyday Life*, "What is Social Intelligence?" we need to ask some related questions about the content and span of social intelligence. For example, we need to assess the extent to which SI depends on the human capacities of feelings or reason, how it evolves through time, and how it is related to or responds to history. We also need to consider how social intelligence accounts for the strong reciprocity that permeates all types of social relations, and the resistance that is presented to those who try to initiate and implement changes.

Two of the most basic questions about social intelligence are covered in the second and third chapters of *Social Intelligence in Everyday Life*: Chapter II, "How is Social Intelligence Learned?" and Chapter III, "What Does Social Intelligence Do For Us?" These questions help us to understand the optimal conditions for increasing social intelligence, as well as the benefits of being socially intelligent.

I. What is Social Intelligence?

After considering how we become socially intelligent, and what the advantages of social intelligence are, the remaining chapters in *Social Intelligence in Everyday Life* try to answer questions such as: what are the risks of having low social intelligence; what are the most important sources of social intelligence; how can we create our own unique blends or versions of social intelligence; how can we encourage others to be socially intelligent or to learn about social intelligence; and what kind of roles can social intelligence play in planning and realizing the future.

These are just a few of the more pressing and interesting questions that we can raise about social intelligence. As we learn more about it, we create more questions and thereby strengthen our abilities to distinguish between those questions that can be answered and those that cannot. Social intelligence is not a ready-made, inherited, or omniscient faculty. There is always more to learn about society and ourselves, and the limits of our human capacities inevitably leave us constantly grappling with more questions and more answers.

A socially intelligent person questions obvious and mundane situations which are either easy to observe, or taken for granted. Questions lead to a deeper understanding of social realities and truths, as well as to sharper perceptions about current conditions and the feasibility of specific goals. Formulating questions exercises and increases social intelligence, and may gradually resolve stresses, or at least reveal how people and social influences really operate.

There is always a story of non-obvious meanings behind the ordinary aspects of our worlds, which can be discovered through applying social intelligence to answer questions on established views. Questions help us to prune the many complexities of social relationships and social influences, so that we may develop clarity and understanding about ourselves and society, and ourselves in society.

II. How is Social
Intelligence Learned?

O ne of the most significant defining characteristics of social intelligence is that it is learned. This means that although SI depends somewhat on innate capacities of understanding and knowing, it is essentially an intellectual and practical skill that is developed throughout life. Social intelligence is both a science and an art of sizing up the particular social situations in which we find ourselves, including the ability to place a wide range of situations in broad social contexts. When we see and act according to the larger picture of our lives, we are practicing social intelligence.

To some extent, social intelligence is learned like anything else we learn. We are what we think is human because we are socialized. It is because we learn the ways of different cultures that we are accepted as full members of our societies. We learn though trial and error, most particularly from making mistakes, and we learn through observing others' behavior. Even listening to media newscasts can be thought of as a way to learn what is expected of us in contemporary society.

What we learn about relationships and society in our earliest years is particularly influential. Our initial impressions of who we are and what our lives are about have the power to orient us for years, sometimes for a lifetime. Although these emotional foundations of our identities and our worldviews can be changed at any time through our actions, they tend to persist and re-emerge, especially in times of stress, crisis, or need, unless we deliberately do things differently. The primary actors in the earliest dramas that contribute to creating who we are, as well as what society is, are members of our families.

When our lessons have an emotional tone, such as principles of right and wrong, the substance of our learning has a deep-seated impact on our behavior. In most instances, moral principles have a strong influence on us because they are instilled by our families, or by our most significant others. Other conditions that influence this kind of deep learning include crises, tragedies, and particularly meaningful occasions.

The fact that we learn social intelligence means that we can also unlearn it. Sometimes our social learning is problematic or dysfunctional. For example, we may learn how to deviate or commit criminal acts from significant others, who necessarily exert strong influences on our lives. However, through changing our understanding of the moral order of society, or of our place in society, we can begin to see things differently, which can ultimately neutralize problematic aspects of negative deep learning.

One way of becoming the human beings we want to be is through deliberately choosing the contexts in which we participate. When we give our attention only to those groups in which we believe, we absorb their values. A clear example of this is deciding to undergo a particular course of study, which eventually gives us the qualifications and way of thinking necessary to holding a specialized job or to becoming a professional.

It is largely from our own experiences—being aware of the social influences involved in the push and pull of our everyday exchanges with others—that we gradually become more socially intelligent. Because of the essential nature of the social influences in our experiences, children under the age of eighteen frequently have inadequate levels of social intelligence. Although some conventional social skills allow adolescents and adults to get by in various social situations, in the long run only social intelligence can serve as a reliable source of guidance for navigating the many complexities of society at large.

Just as it is important for young adults to become sufficiently aware of the broad social influences that most affect their lives, learning social intelligence should ideally continue throughout one's lifetime. As career paths change, and social conditions are transformed throughout our global society, people at all stages of the life cycle need to observe and understand how broad social influences affect their lives. Transitions to old age and death are intense social experiences that should be continually reassessed by members of each generation.

When we understand how social intelligence can be learned, we take charge of our lives more easily. As we continue to learn SI we can choose directions to follow more independently, and we are more likely to be the people we really want to be. This level of awareness benefits society as a whole because we increase our abilities to act as effective human agents when we know where we stand in relation to social traditions, resources, and values.

Early Impressions

Many of our childhood memories are directly related to people and events that opened up our protected worlds. Through birthday parties when we were young, for example, we begin to develop a sense of self and of having some kind of social position among our friends. Although as children we must depend on our family members for direction and sustenance, we gradually become participants in a world that is much bigger than our families. When we are young, however, most of our impressions of society are filtered through our parents' perceptions and activities. At first we see only who we are, our friends, and limited social situations through the eyes of our parents, siblings, and significant others.

Even when these kinds of early impressions are vague, they are important in that they begin to create a foundation for our understanding of what society is all about, and how we fit into this social context. Because of the central importance of these early impressions, it behooves us to articulate what we think or imagine our earliest impressions are, while at the same time making deliberate efforts to strengthen our social intelligence as adults.

One of the lasting consequences of our early impressions of social influences is that we develop a specific posture to life. This habitual orientation is typically either relatively positive and accepting of our part in society as a whole, or more negative because it includes awareness of a contradiction between who we think we are and how others see or deal with us as we go about our daily lives.

Whatever posture to life these early impressions help us to develop, our resulting dominant perspectives strongly influence our behavior, goals, and life outcomes.

If our earliest impressions have destructive influences on our orientations to the world, we need to work hard to change some of the values that we internalized as youngsters. Our early impressions are powerful, but not omnipotent, and we can modify them and their impact on our behavior through a variety of techniques. For example, we might have imitated our fathers' conventional approach to choosing a career, due to early childhood influences. However, when we learn how to assess our own interests and opportunities more skillfully, deliberate applications of wisely selected strategies will allow us to move beyond our fathers' limiting biases.

Early impressions connect us to the past and to older family members. One advantage of early impressions is that they are markers of particular historical times, relationships, and events so they can help us to make sense of our past, present, and future. These impressions become indicators of some of the main themes of our lives, and they lay the groundwork for building more sophisticated kinds of social intelligence.

Gender role expectations are another powerful aspect of what we learn from our early impressions. We quickly accept relatives' examples of how to be a man or a woman, and we do not immediately see many of the important and subtle gender differences that can be chosen and nurtured when we gain a deeper understanding of who we are and what society is. However, even when we are effectively being responsible for our own gender socialization, we still tend to be haunted and influenced by our earliest impressions. Such impressions continue to be powerful influences on our social intelligence, regardless of the steps we take in adult life to create and express our authentic selves.

We need to find a conscious starting point for developing our social intelligence, perhaps at a relatively arbitrary time, if we are to grow effectively and become more mature. It would be nice to have nothing but constructive early impressions about who we are and what society is, but this is usually not possible. Of more significance, however, is that some of our early impressions become a resource or foundation for learning more useful kinds of social intelligence.

II. How is Social Intelligence Learned?

Deep Learning

When we are young, or merely naive about particular social situations, we learn from our experiences with an unquestioning attitude. This innocence and openness facilitates a deep kind of learning. Deep learning is also different from the academic learning mandated by educational institutions. Instead of regurgitating others' ideas, deep learning carves out more personalized ideas, values, and beliefs in our psyches and souls, which are often difficult to ignore or remove.

Imitation is a significant means of learning deeply. When we are young, or even at later ages, we watch and identify with family members or people we admire. Even though we may be oblivious to many of the nuances in this process, sooner or later we find that we are becoming similar to those we admire, or, even to those of whom we are afraid. Wherever there is a strong and meaningful emotional bond between the learner and the person observed, there is a tendency for this kind of identification and imitation to take place. Only by deliberately becoming our own selves can we halt or control this inclination, because then we can be more selective about whom we allow to influence our thoughts and actions. If we are too emotionally close to others, through relationships based largely on love, dislike, hatred, or care-taking, we are less able to achieve independence.

Social intelligence shows us that deep learning produces both positive and negative influences in our lives. We absorb constructive patterns of behavior, which inspire and protect us, as well as destructive patterns of behavior, which may ultimately destroy us as well as others. Only by practicing our power in choosing how we allow deep learning to influence our lives can we stop being victims of harmful deep learning. SI helps us to discriminate between positive and negative deep learning influences. When we translate our dreams into strategies to expedite constructive deep learning, we take charge of our destinies, and move more quickly toward making worthwhile contributions to the common good.

One of the unwanted influences of deep learning is that it strengthens our capacities to get through our daily business on automatic pilot. We are conditioned by our deep learning, and we do what we do more easily because of the substructures of our deep learning. Thus deep learning can encourage complacency with the status quo, and make us less critical of our behavior patterns. However, when we change our deep learning through practicing social intelligence, we are more alert and deliberate in whatever we choose to do.

In all, deep learning and automatic behavior can also create noteworthy benefits. Having good manners ingrained in us through deep learning, for example, improves how we relate to others so that we do not need to think through what we should do each time we make a move. Thus we can depend on some of our deeply learned patterns of behavior, and we benefit from them largely because they are automatic. In many respects, our deep learning creates those habits or strategies that we take for granted and often think of as "instinctive" or "natural."

Social intelligence is composed of and guided by whatever we learn at deep levels, as well as influenced by what we learn in more cognitive, intellectual ways. In comparing these two modes of learning, however, we should acknowledge that deep learning frequently has a stronger influence on our behavior than formal education. Therefore it is difficult to change long-established patterns of thinking, being, and doing—including that behavior which intellectually we know we should modify for our own good and for the good of others. With persistence and ingenuity, deep learning can be modified in the long run, especially when the original deep learning is replaced by more constructive or acceptable patterns of behavior.

A crisis is one of the most auspicious situations for initiating deep learning as a means of increasing social intelligence. Whatever the unfortunate circumstances of a particular crisis are, it is possible to use challenging or destructive experiences of dislocation as opportunities to learn something new and important that will serve as a guide for years to come. Upon the loss of a parent, for example, we can decide to carry on the work of that parent, or to further some of the habits and values of the lost parent. A different kind of response to this loss is to become sufficiently freed up to make decisions that were previously too difficult to make. Furthermore, in times of political or social upheaval such as war or rapid social change, we will become more secure by deliberately cultivating goals to increase social stability, or to contribute to a newly defined common good. Social intelligence increases whenever we deal thoughtfully with crises on any level.

II. How is Social Intelligence Learned?

Unlearning

When we reach a certain age, whether young adulthood or middle age, we frequently become painfully aware that we are not who we want to be, and we have not accomplished even a semblance of our dreams. We might find, for example, that although we followed fairly religiously what our parents, friends, or teachers told us to do through the years, we have reached a disappointing impasse where we do not enjoy life or find as much meaning in our daily activities as we believe we should. At such a point of frustration, or even despair, we can begin to identify the futility of some of our habitual efforts to find fulfillment, and at the same time do something to change our behavior. Similarly, if we feel we are stuck at crossroads that never disappear, or if we feel trapped in ruts that claim our freedom and imagination, we may begin to realize that life need not be this way. These signs become our invitation to unlearn what we have learned to date, and to build the kind of social intelligence that will guide us more effectively without letting us down.

Individual dissatisfaction is frequently a precondition for much of the unlearning that people decide to do. This chain of events is activated because we are not inclined to undergo the difficult tasks necessary to make changes in who we are, unless we have clear and painful evidence that our lives are not working out the way we want. Furthermore, if our discomfort is not acute, we may merely tell ourselves that all we need to do is to try harder, make a fresh start, or turn over a new leaf, rather than unlearn who we are. When it is too difficult to work up sufficient motivation to make substantial changes in our lives, the relatively minor adaptations we try to make frequently do not work in the long run. Unlearning is a major enterprise that takes a great deal of time and energy, but it is often the only means we have for reaching our goals.

Deliberately unlearning our past conditioning changes our values and priorities, which enables us to go in new directions. This sea change affects our behavior and the decisions we make. One condition for the success of unlearning processes is that we must take them very seriously if they are to be effective. Furthermore, we frequently cannot remove negative things that we have learned without replacing them with something else. When we make a deliberate effort to increase our social intelligence, the "something else" which is substituted needs to be more beneficial than what had been previously learned. Unlearning cannot create such a substitution or function effectively from a vacuum, and we are compelled to come up with some kind of rationale for whatever is being unlearned and learned.

Social intelligence enables us to know what we need to unlearn, and to take strategic steps to change our conditioned reactions and responses. We need to deliberately open ourselves up to new ideas and to practice innovative strategies. Whether or not we are aware of what SI is, we can decide to sort out our lives, so that we become more effective agents and players in our lives. In contrast to the trial and error modes of getting our acts together, deliberate unlearning increases our social intelligence more directly, so that we can more truly take charge of our lives.

When we use social intelligence we may first target what we do not want to do, such as waste time and energy in meaningless activities, before we move toward the behavior, goals, and lifestyle we want to accomplish. Effective unlearning is a process whereby we weed out what we do not want to do, and at the same time plant the seeds and take the actions necessary for moving in our preferred directions. These two steps are more congruent when we use our social intelligence to develop a clear vision of what we ultimately want to do in the context of broader society.

We necessarily reorganize our time and energy as we unlearn our most unproductive thoughts and activities. These actions increase our social intelligence beyond the level of SI we had when we first saw our need for unlearning and developed some effective unlearning strategies. Our SI continues to increase through combining our unlearning with new learning. Thus unlearning gives us added control over our negative or dysfunctional patterns of behavior, which may have been instilled in our childhood or in times of crisis, and it is through successful unlearning that we move ahead more freely to tackle bigger projects and make commitments to broader purposes.

Learning Contexts

Because a large proportion of our social intelligence is based on learning from our experiences, the particular contexts in which we find ourselves are crucial in defining the content and meanings we absorb. Our attitudes, values, and patterns of thinking respond or react to our social surroundings, and specific aspects of these contexts—such as emotional climates, power dynamics, and relationships—are strong influences on what we learn, and on our social intelligence.

The more we are in charge of ourselves the more we can deliberately select the environments in which we spend our time and energy. If we are religious, for example, we can choose to participate in the church or synagogue congregation we value most. Similarly, if we want to learn a profession, we can register for courses of instruction or attend workshops that will help us to realize our long-term goals. We trust that we are sufficiently talented to benefit from these contexts, and during the process of relating to those who are in the same situation, we become more socially intelligent.

Our families are among the most significant learning contexts we can choose. We are emotionally enmeshed in our closest relationships, whether or not we realize it, and becoming more objective about our most personal bonds enables us to act more freely. Our interdependencies need to be explored, not ignored or denied, and we do this successfully only by remaining vigilant about how we interact with our relatives. Our position in our familial dependencies is a measure of our social intelligence, and what we can do to change it.

Another context of our learning and social intelligence is our memberships in a range of different social classes. We respond and are responded to variously, depending on our economic status, race, ethnicity, gender, sexual orientation, or physical abilities. Pressures to conform to group or class traditions sometimes make it difficult to be individuals in our own right within these contexts. Limited social intelligence all too often flows from the expectations of these groups or classes, rather than from our own individual beliefs and integrity. We benefit more and we further increase our social intelligence, when we decide how we will respond to these class pressures to conform, and cultivate our own individualized responses to what others think of us.

The culture of society—shared values, standards, norms, and beliefs—is another powerful context of our learning. If we live in societies with high levels of consumerism, for example, materialistic influences will form the context of many of our life choices. We need to develop means—through social intelligence—which help us to rise above popular cultural standards, so that we can meet our personal needs as well as collective needs for life-satisfaction more effectively. We are cultural beings, and civilization is based on culture, but we need not become victims of specific cultural limitations. Social intelligence helps us to see culture for what it is, and to respond more thoughtfully to these cultural strengths and limitations.

Society itself is another significant context for learning social intelligence. The more complex a society is, the more complex our social intelligence is. This is because we absorb the structures, content, and processes of society at our deepest levels of being. One caveat here, however, is that we must realize that many preliterate societies, which may appear to be relatively simple, usually have multiple layers of cultural and structural complexity that are not readily apparent to contemporary observers. Whatever the societal context, social patterns are embedded within individual and social consciousness within a particular society.

Economic and political conditions in society also affect the kind of social intelligence that is transmitted or cultivated in society at large. In times of economic depression, recession, or prosperity, different kinds of individual and social awareness develop. Similarly, war and peace are determining influences on social intelligence. We may be negative or positive in orientation, for example, largely as a result of these particular emotional climates, possibilities, and opportunities.

Experience

If we are to learn anything, we must be teachable. This means that we need to entertain others' ideas seriously, and to be open to the impact of external influences that challenge our assumptions about reality and about who we are. Above all, we are taught through our exchanges with other people, and we are affected by the totality of our everyday experiences. No experience leaves us without some kind of mark or effect.

Even when we merely take our own observations and reflections seriously, our unique perceptions have the power to challenge the kinds of things we habitually take for granted about physical, emotional, and social realities. For example, when we try to accomplish certain goals, we inevitably get some kind of feedback from our environment as to whether or not we are

II. How is Social Intelligence Learned?

actually attaining these objectives. It is not possible for us to escape or perpetually deny the situations we are in, however hard we may try. We cannot interpret our circumstances optimistically, or solely according to our own points of view or interests indefinitely. Unless we completely block out the realities of our day-to-day existence, which would be counterproductive, our experiences will force us to reassess what we are about and where we are headed.

Experience is life itself, and it inevitably involves our entire being. For example, we are emotionally connected to other people, whether we know them or not and whether we believe this fact or not; mutuality influences all our behavior. Therefore, even though we may not choose to be conventional in our outlooks or habitual behavior, we are dogged by others' views of us. Whether or not we respect the people we are with, and whether or not we pay attention to others as we go about our everyday routines, what we do and experience is strongly influenced by our immediate interdependencies, and even by those we do not know. Group emotions and group pressures are powerful whether they are positive or negative: families tie their members into their shared expectations in some of the same ways that the level of violence in a city influences how individuals conduct themselves.

One way to start liberating ourselves from this emotional reactivity between people is to make conscious efforts to develop our social intelligence as we go about our daily chores. When we express ourselves emotionally as well as intellectually in what we do, and understand some of the social sources of what motivates our own and others' actions, we become more objective in our attitudes and behavior. Seeing the pressures of reciprocity in our interactions allows us to get some distance from the power and negative consequences of these bonds and expectations.

Our experiences are deeply influenced by the qualities of the feelings we have, and specific social conditions sometimes provoke very strong emotional responses. We may identify strongly with specific communities and their goals, for instance, and at the same time experience uncomfortable alienation from other groups. The feelings experienced are often not generated by qualities of personality, but rather are the combined effects or interplay of our social intelligence and our particular situations. Thus our social intelligence filters our social experiences. It is our

27

SI that determines how and why we allow some stimuli to influence us, while others are relatively excluded from our awareness. It intensifies our sensitivity to desired objectives, such as creating meaningful family relationships, and at the same time strengthens our immunity to influences that we do not want to affect us, such as rivalry on the job.

Experiential learning is sometimes thought of as indelible, and we sometimes consider intuition to be an effective means to know what is most important to us in our everyday experiences. However, experiential learning is not fixed, and it is our social intelligence that essentially guides our intuition. SI helps us not to become victims of our feelings, and it shows us how to use our intuition and feelings to understand complexities in our individual and social realities, so that we can act in more enlightened ways.

Another aspect of the link between social intelligence and experience, and how we learn social intelligence, is the inevitability of having a social class membership. It is helpful to know what our social class is, for example, if we are stuck in deciding which goals to follow in our careers or personal lives. Also, we need to become sufficiently free from the traditions of our particular social class origins, so that we can do something other than merely meet others' class expectations. Social intelligence helps us to be astute and autonomous with regard to the powerful overt or hidden social pressures that structure and sometimes dominate both our small group milieus and our more global environments.

Lifetime Learning

Although the capacity to be socially intelligent is necessary for survival, the content and dimensions of our SI at different ages depend on our earliest social contacts, our continuing dependencies, the situations with which we have to cope, and our unique experiences. Furthermore, social intelligence is learned over the whole of a lifetime rather than inherited. We become socially intelligent in order to survive, and even though SI defines the quality of much of our existence on a day-to-day basis, the kind of social intelligence we develop is not preordained in any way.

The fact that we need social intelligence to survive throughout our lifetimes means that this human characteristic is malleable. Like the perennial challenge to build character, we are faced with the ongoing challenge to continue to nurture our social intelligence. Whereas character is frequently thought of as priorities and qualities that may be largely latent rather than manifest, different facets of social intelligence are needed and expressed at every turn of events. SI helps us to take care of our needs as infants and as elderly persons; it allows us to take others into account in some way in every decision we make. Deliberately using social intelligence provides us with a practical, optimistic view of ourselves and our opportunities, so that we can orient and implement all our actions more effectively. Although character is usually best understood through looking at a person's behavior over long periods of time, most particularly in crises, social intelligence is largely an expression of applied knowledge in our everyday behavior. Because of its practicality, SI can be thought of as feeding into the construction of character, and perhaps even as its lifeblood.

Social intelligence is a means to size up the complexities of all kinds of social conditions as they present themselves to us on a continuing basis. Over a lifetime, SI becomes a seasoned, sophisticated guide upon which we can call for direction. However, it may not always be fully expressed in our actions, even though ideally it is a source of wisdom that gives us sufficient understanding to allow our empathy or ideals to move us. Thus when we are adults, we can look back to assess which parts of our lives were guided by social intelligence, and which were more or less lived automatically, without making adequate use of our social intelligence.

Social intelligence protects and preserves us at different stages of the life cycle. We become increasingly aware, for example, of how to protect ourselves, or of how to express ourselves regardless of others' pressures to do what they want. Even though many people are motivated to act in their own interests, social intelligence tempers blind ambition, and at best moves us toward making direct contributions to the common good, especially in relation to achieving long-range goals. Thus SI may help us to stay on a moral high ground, while at the same time making us more immune to the push and pull of others' non-rational demands.

In addition to living with purpose through using social intelligence, we need to learn how to die effectively. SI can guide us to deliberately build a heritage to leave to others. For example, we develop socially intelligent habits over the years, so that we do not succumb to pressures that dissipate our vital energies. Valuing what social intelligence suggests at every stage of life helps us to stay in charge of what we want to do with our lives. Getting lost in the crowd, or acting as cheerful robots, wastes our time and energy so that we cannot make the world a better place. Social intelligence shows us how to answer a higher calling of purpose and direction that enables us to build something of lasting value for the next generation.

III. What Does Social Intelligence Do For Us?

S ocial intelligence bestows many rich advantages. In historical or traditional contexts, it is similar to wisdom. However, because so many moral or religious connotations are associated with wisdom, it is perhaps more accurate to think of social intelligence—in contrast to wisdom—as being more firmly rooted in experience than in ancient treatises, religious texts, or classical literature. In addition, social intelligence is more inextricably and directly caught up with meeting the challenges of modern day society than is wisdom, which, in its timelessness, can be more ambiguous.

In spite of these important contrasts, both wisdom and social intelligence can enhance or increase meaning and purpose in everyday life for most people. All other things being equal, we prefer to be wise or socially intelligent because we know that we are more likely to make the right decisions as we go about our daily business.

Social intelligence can benefit all, regardless of who we are, where we are, and what our particular circumstances are. This is because SI wakes us up to the power of those social realities in our lives that affect us the most. Furthermore, it is our social intelligence which enables us to find answers to the big questions which haunt us: what is of most importance to us, what blocks our abilities to be productive, and what we can do to improve our present situations.

Social intelligence informs us at all stages of our everyday decision-making, and at the same time helps us to articulate our most cherished goals and ideals. SI makes it possible for us to

31

balance reason and emotion in our actions, in part because the learned talent of social intelligence allows us to see the larger picture of who we are in society at large, and what we can best do to be effective. By helping us to discern and understand the many social complexities which influence us, it also deepens our awareness of the tensions that necessarily exist between ourselves and groups at all social levels, from local to global.

The essence of social intelligence can also be compared with maturity. We can make more knowledgeable assessments of ourselves and what we want to do with our lives when we allow it to guide our understanding of what is, and to clarify our vision of what might be. Because social intelligence sharpens our sense of purpose, we can depend on it to guide us toward accomplishing our most meaningful goals.

To the extent that we achieve solid successes in our lives by pursuing these cherished goals and ideals, we make sound investments in our shared future and create valuable legacies for those who follow us. On a more personal level, social intelligence also strengthens us against the sabotage of our adversaries by increasing our immunity to others' pressures and manipulations.

Social intelligence improves the quality of our lives in many mundane ways because it is a dependable source of enlightenment for the most basic tasks we must accomplish during our lifetimes: education, work, personal and professional commitments, family responsibilities, and contributions to the common good. When we accomplish these tasks successfully, we develop our unique potentials and are more able to have satisfying, long-lasting relationships.

Increases Awareness

Social intelligence strengthens a person's capacity to be objective about self, others, and society. In doing so, SI makes us more aware of who we are, or seem to be, from others' viewpoints as well as our own; it also puts what we want to do with our lives in the broadest social contexts possible. We are who we are, and we want to do what we want to do, because we are products of the societies where we live or have lived. Furthermore, each society has its own place in the world at large.

Even though social intelligence takes into account how others see us, it does not suggest that this awareness means that we have to act or react directly to others' views. Rather, we benefit from distinguishing and respecting the fact that how we see ourselves frequently differs dramatically from how others see us. We need to separate these views in order to act autonomously, rather than to merely please others or conform to their expectations. Awareness is a powerful habit of the mind, and we are more able to exercise our true options when we can first see what they are.

The awareness brought about through our social intelligence allows us to see, at any time, the broad panoramas of our lives, as well as the subtle and not so subtle intricacies of our dependencies on others. Once we are awakened to the presence and strength of social influences in our daily exchanges with others, however, we must remain vigilant as to how they affect what we think and what we do. The imprints of our social bonds and conditioning are pervasive and never leave us alone. If we think or believe that we are solitary actors, we delude ourselves.

One significant way in which social intelligence increases our awareness is that it helps us to realize what our values are, how much we are committed to them, and to what extent our values are expressed in our day-to-day behavior. We can begin to become more effective in whatever we want to accomplish when we make deliberate efforts to articulate and actualize the values and priorities in which we really believe. Thus our social intelligence guides us to be more consistent in our beliefs and actions, and this kind of consolidated awareness firms up our base of action, making us more able to attain the goals we set for ourselves.

Social intelligence also helps us to be continually aware of our personal boundaries and the boundaries of others. We become more respectful of our own and others' limitations when we are aware of where we draw the line in defining the responsibilities we assume. When we have this degree of awareness, we are in a better position to recognize and pay attention to the internal and external messages of our feelings, intuitions, and bodily reactions. Our feelings do not occur only from within ourselves. Our emotions and passions are inextricably tied and meaningfully connected to our social environments and the emotional climates in which we act on a daily basis.

The awareness we gain from social intelligence enables us to see and know the power of the strongest social influences in our lives. Without this awareness, we are all too easily pushed and pulled in many different directions, including in those ways that we do not want or choose for ourselves. However, when we use SI to assess the various situations we get into, we are more aware of the pressures of social class, gender, normative standards, and other social and emotional systems that have a strong impact on how we live. Deliberately cultivating this kind of awareness or enlightenment through becoming more socially intelligent enables us to choose more freely to be who we really want to be, and to do what we really want to do.

Clarifies Vision

Social intelligence helps us to see the facts of our particular social situations and the course of our lives. It is not useful to get so carried away with hopes and dreams—a kind of romance—that we do not face up to facts. Since social realities are such a powerful part of the influences defining the conditions of our existence, assessing our situations through making use of social intelligence clears the way for seeing our true possibilities.

It is only when we understand where our starting points are, what they mean, and who we are as social beings, that we can seriously consider what our priorities are or should be. SI helps us to establish or re-establish our priorities because it enables us to assess more accurately what is important to us as we conduct our lives. It also helps us to take stock of what has gone on in our past, what is happening in our present, and what could be in our future. Thus social intelligence is a means or a technique that helps us to focus on what we really want to accomplish, and how we can build our future on our accomplishments. Social intelligence also helps us to learn from the mistakes we have made, and shows us how to avoid damaging repetitions of unproductive behavior that does not take social circumstances into account.

Social intelligence guides us in monitoring the real nature of our daily transactions, so that we can have clearer priorities in what we try to do on a daily basis. Deliberately cultivating clear visions of our goals helps us to see our options in perspective, and helps us to make the often-difficult choices that constantly confront us. It is imperative that we be able to see what is important to us at all times—and social intelligence allows us to do this—if we are to eventually accomplish that which is the most meaningful to us.

The clarity of vision made possible by social intelligence not only enhances our capacities to formulate goals and future

III. What Does Social Intelligence Do For Us?

possibilities, but also extends our awareness of the necessity of incorporating the welfare of others in our objectives. When clarity of vision is strengthened by social intelligence, our perspective becomes inclusive rather than ethnocentric. This is because SI shows us that the well-being of each individual is inextricably tied to the well-being of the whole. We cannot afford to be self-serving in our visions of the future, because this will inevitably destroy the group in the long run, thus bringing about our own demise.

In addition to fostering these important dimensions of shared social realities, social intelligence directs us away from egotistical self-interest to a deepened appreciation of our own individual creativity. Unique genius can save the world regardless of whether it is artistic talent, scientific discovery, technological invention, or individual expression. Our visions of these kinds of possibilities, when informed by social intelligence, are truly distinctive because of the influence of our own values and experiences; they are also truly liberating with respect to given social needs. SI helps us to see the complex ranges and levels of social realities, which span individual circumstances, global conditions, and evolution. We are creatures of history who have only one life to live within these awesome parameters.

Social intelligence, rather than restricting our options, enables us to be more discriminating in selecting what our visions of the past and present in the future are. SI enables us to more effectively decide what we should be doing with our day-to-day lives. It is this quality of ordinariness that enables us all to consider the power and significance of our attitudes and postures to action, as well as our behavior. Do we go along with others for no real reason or stay our ground? Do we act on principle, or do we agree to be pushed along with the flow?

When social intelligence makes it possible for us to increase the clarity of our visions, the effectiveness of our present behavior is also increased. When we know where we are headed, our activities are more goal-directed as well as more meaningful. We are able to build visions that last longer, for example, because SI helps us to incorporate the power of social processes into our goals. Having constructed such visions, we are more objective about the circumstances we face and must overcome. We do not as easily allow pessimism to sway us from proceeding in the direction of our visions, and consequently we are more productive in whatever we choose to do.

Increases Purpose

One of the most significant things that social intelligence does for us is to increase purpose in our actions. When we cultivate it, through learning as much as we can about ourselves in the world about us, we both clarify our visions of what can be and increase our senses of purpose in our everyday exchanges with others. It is easiest to strengthen our missions when we really know where we are going.

Purpose is increased because when we know what it is that we truly, in social conscience, want to achieve, we can at last proceed hopefully, patiently, steadfastly, and meaningfully in that same direction. When we are focused in this way, our daily actions, however minuscule they may seem, lead us more surely toward our ultimate goals. Furthermore, even though we may not appear to be making much progress toward accomplishing whatever our visions of possibilities are, we will have more peace of mind from having harnessed our energies in these ways, and from having made the effort to proceed in this direction. We are most successful in this endeavor when we deliberately allow ourselves to be guided and directed at all stages of our enterprises by our social intelligence. Using SI enables us to be more enlightened in our actions.

Social intelligence, because it is grounded in social realities, makes our aims, and our senses of purpose, more sure. For example, when we face up to the power of the complex social influences in our lives, we are less likely to be waylaid by fads, fashions, and pressures, even by those which flow from the most eminent of social sources. Because of the inextricable relatedness of this chain of effects, increasing our social intelligence predictably increases the degree of our purposeful single-mindedness in our day-to-day lives.

Social intelligence governs our behavior and the quality of our everyday life to a great extent, whether or not we knowingly allow its guidance and direction. However, we can derive many advantages from realizing these inextricable associations. For example, when we understand society more fully, we know ourselves more deeply, as well as our dearest goals, and the conditions essential for their accomplishment. Thus, when we specify our goals by using our social intelligence, our purposes increase, as well as our motivations to succeed. Understanding social complexities gives us sufficient confidence to design effective purposes and strategies, which in turn allow us to transcend the barriers and obstacles that inevitably come our way.

Broad perspectives and new meanings are derived from applying social intelligence to particular situations, and these enable us to be more committed to our courses of action, and more dedicated to achieving our most cherished goals and their related outcomes. Innovative, creative directions generated by social intelligence foster new kinds of purpose, and this deepened commitment carries us further in our intentions.

These important byproducts of exercising social intelligence increase our persistence, as we take action to accomplish our goals, and our competence in finding effective ways to deal with the difficulties inherent in our particular social circumstances. Furthermore, social intelligence shows us how our purposes and goals are influenced by social systems, social classes, and values. Ideally, we are constantly learning through undertaking meaningful quests, and when we act in alignment with our purposes we strengthen our social intelligence.

Although increasing purpose may not seem important when we carefully scrutinize how we really want to live, we can perhaps see that doing something meaningful brings richer personal and social rewards than having a passive, apathetic existence. When we allow ourselves to drift through the years, following social dictates haphazardly, it is easy to lose zest and enthusiasm, and to become a dilettante or dabbler rather than an actor. When we do this, we numb ourselves to historical social realities, and become the pawns of others without knowing what we are doing or what we are missing.

Guides and Directs

Social intelligence guides and directs us in our observations, decisions, and behavior whether or not we are aware of this guidance and direction. We can deliberately rely on social intelligence as a source of guidance and direction because it is essentially a body of knowledge, principles, skills, and practical know-how about the world we live in. Social intelligence is a valuable frame of reference that both represents and responds to our lived experiences, and at the same time allows us to have a meaningful perspective on whatever is going on in our lives. When we understand the social contexts of who we are, and identify the social influences which exert pressures on different aspects of our being, we can more fully appreciate why we behave in the ways we do.

Because we are constantly accumulating and consolidating our social intelligence from our ongoing observations, experiences, and education, our SI grows throughout our life-course and is readily accessible whenever we need it. We can call upon it to guide us in whatever circumstances we find ourselves at all times. Experientially speaking, our social intelligence is a dependable guide that directs us in constructive ways in spite of the hurly-burly of everyday life.

We can rely on social intelligence for guidance and direction because its facts and meanings include wisdom as well as knowledge, and because it has proved its usefulness through time, to us personally and to our civilizations. Our humanity is a product of our social intelligence, and our greatest leaders have used their social intelligence to achieve important and necessary social goals. Most people have at least some capacity to learn and understand social realities, so that they benefit consciously or unconsciously from its guidance.

Social intelligence can not only be applied to achieving our goals and objectives, but also to understanding what we can reasonably expect from others, and how we can best be prepared to deal with their resistance, conflict of interests, and pressures to behave in contradictory ways. SI makes us more realistic when we formulate plans for our lives, as well as when we try to build relationships with others.

In the process of using our social intelligence we can see more clearly what the links are between our values, the social structures of society, and our behavior. It is important to remember that we are socially conditioned at deep levels merely to even become human in the first place; consequently we are socially influenced in whatever we think and do. Because we are unable to eliminate the many different kinds of social pressures we face on a daily basis, our most sensible option is to try to understand them, making deliberate use of this knowledge in the choices we make about conducting our everyday lives. When we use social intelligence to guide and direct our behavior, we are no longer as vulnerable to being pressured by others. This means that when we consciously let it guide and direct us, we are able to live more fully.

III. What Does Social Intelligence Do For Us?

As social intelligence relates to our families, religions or beliefs, economic, educational, and political systems, it enhances our awareness of how we are connected to the roots of our societies. Our SI is one of the deepest and most influential sources of our individual and social identities; it places us in meaningful social contexts. Thus it shows us where we belong in response to our deep-seated needs for community, rather than cuts us off from others, which inevitably creates the kinds of conditions that produce or increase alienation.

Invests in the Future

Because social intelligence consistently helps us to come to terms with the past and to live more fully in the present, cultivating it is one of our best investments for the future. We learn how to be socially intelligent throughout our lives, and this learning never ceases. We learn how to die well in the same way that we learn how to live more effectively.

When we are children, or when we raise our children and grandchildren, we face the future while taking the present and past into account. However, unless episodes from the past erupt into our present, we often do not give much attention to whatever has happened previously. But always the unknowns of the future lure us on, or strike terror in us. The future is a mysterious presence in most people's lives, as they go about picking up pieces of the past and dealing with present challenges on a daily basis.

Social intelligence guides and directs us toward the future we want, and it serves us as a resource when we find that we are confronted with the unexpected, the feared, and the unknown. It is our enlightenment, support, inspiration, and refuge. We can depend on social intelligence to give us good, dependable ideas, and to be there for us whatever comes our way.

Social intelligence helps us to recognize and understand what is going on in the wider society and the global community. This is particularly true today when near and distant social trends accelerate to such a pitch that they bring about unprecedented shifts in the familiar social arrangements of our own societies. We can be at peace one minute and at war the next, for example, and usually neither one of these very significant social and emotional conditions seems to be of our own making. SI helps us to deal with even such dramatically transformed circumstances, so that we can remain strong and independent in our adaptations as changes continue around us.

The likelihood of making successful adaptations to rapid social changes is due to our being able to use social intelligence in identifying important social trends, and assessing their significance in the world. We cannot be in advantageous positions in a society without maintaining a high level of awareness and alertness about our external surroundings and our many different relationships. When we understand these basic social conditions of our situations, we are much strengthened and better able to be directed by our own ideals and principles.

Enlightenment through social intelligence shows us to what extent we can or may want to participate in ongoing social changes. For example, we may choose to be directed and guided by it to initiate actions and strategies that work toward enhancing the common good. SI helps us to understand, explain, and predict social change, and to see ourselves as agents of change within shifting trends. We become historical actors and invest in the future when we use social intelligence to move with the times, while addressing vital social issues that emerge in the present. In many respects, SI is a tool for creating or maintaining optimal social conditions for as many people as possible in society in the present and future.

Social intelligence propels us in these constructive and idealistic directions when we make thorough use of the wisdom and maturity of judgment that is available to us. By concentrating on SI's principles and ideals, we make the world a better place, while increasing our satisfaction with our everyday lives. We also become more valuable family members when we face the future realistically and communicate the best of our lessons to the next generation. Being socially intelligent empowers our capacities to bring about needed changes for the future; our most worthwhile investment for the future is to continuously concentrate on increasing our own social intelligence.

Creates a Legacy

Social intelligence can guide us to create and achieve something of lasting value, which can benefit the common good now and in the years ahead. This kind of legacy may be concrete in kind, such as works of art; or abstract, such as articulating a worthwhile goal for others to achieve. When we express our supreme values through our actions, we can be assured that if these flow from the principles of social intelligence they will create a beneficial legacy.

By allowing SI to guide and direct our behavior, we know beyond a shadow of a doubt, that whatever we produce will sustain others as well as ourselves. When we have a clear vision of our goals, our increased sense of purpose enables us to transcend barriers and obstacles, so that we can be more effective as we negotiate and create beneficial legacies. Thus our socially intelligent awareness serves us as a guide in providing legacies of worthwhile community contributions.

Social intelligence gives us knowledge of the best of all possible worlds; at the same time it yields practical pointers about how we can get there. Having social know-how makes us alert to the many different opportunities that present themselves for achieving a goal or a legacy of increasing the common good. Through SI, we learn how we can make unique contributions in personal, cultural, social, and historical contexts. We become more fully human when we nurture our social intelligence, and we also develop our human potential when we are socially intelligent. We see how our values fit in with, or differ, from those held by various social groups, or by mainstream society, and we become freer in choosing which values we will express in our legacies.

Acting with social intelligence is a form of responsible action that is grounded in the past, present, and future. Our only capacity and possibility is to create the legacies we want now, because when we are dead we have no more power or influence to make a difference. We need to learn what it means to work on our legacies today, and what we must do now to enrich our legacies.

Creating a legacy may seem to be a dull or an overly challenging project, especially with view to our more usual inclinations to rest and relax through the multitude of ways available to us to enjoy ourselves. However, we can be assured that we will have increased life satisfaction when we embark on journeys to create our legacies. Having the design and creation of a meaningful legacy as an objective helps us to get out of bed in the morning, and increases the quality of all our daily exchanges. When we set the goal of putting a legacy in motion, we enjoy life more, become enthusiastic, and act with more verve and zest. Our sense of purpose increases, and we are able to transcend many of the harsh conditions of our day-to-day existence because we know that what we do now will ultimately benefit others. We will not reach the end of this journey to create a legacy, but we merely need to start the journey and make some progress toward what we believe are our best legacies.

Our family and community responsibilities will also be met more fully and satisfactorily when we focus on creating a legacy. Social intelligence shows us that we need to stay connected to our families and communities, but that this attachment should be flexible, outward looking to society, and forward looking to the future. We need to act as whole human beings in our families and with respect to the future. We come full circle in our purposes when we concentrate on doing whatever is needed in order to create our most beneficial legacies. We are responsible for the future as well as for the present, and we will inevitably leave a legacy of some kind, whether we plan it or not. However, the more we focus on the task of building a constructive legacy, the more we will be able to contribute toward making the world a better place.

IV. The Perils of Having Low Social Intelligence

M any dire individual and social consequences may flow from our refusals to deliberately cultivate our social intelligence. When we remain unaware of the power of the social influences molding our living conditions, we risk everything from being pushed around mercilessly by others and losing our priceless independence, to reducing our interest in staying alive and decreasing our power as individuals. If we do not regularly exercise our social intelligence, we are easily lured into spending decades, or even a lifetime, filling artificially constructed roles, living without authenticity, and desperately trying to meet others' expectations before anything else. Having low social intelligence means that we predictably react and behave automatically, so that we eventually miss out on the most vital and most exhilarating purposes of our existence.

When we are not aware of our social intelligence, or what it can be and can do for us, we communicate with others poorly, and we fall short in our understanding of social situations and in our abilities to deal effectively with complex social realities. Unless we deliberately develop our social intelligence, we become increasingly incompetent in our actions; we no longer act decisively or in accordance with our own long-term interests, and we are slow to discern or to create opportunities to cooperate with others.

Therefore, as a consequence, we can become stuck in unpleasant, perhaps dangerous situations. Penalties from having low social intelligence include being unable to make decisions about significant areas of day-to-day life, such as a job or a relationship, and finding it difficult or impossible to act without the urging of others. The long-term impact of these self-destructive patterns of behavior suggests that it is imperative for us to increase our SI if we are to be strong, capable, and effective political or historical agents in our rapidly changing world.

Another peril of having low social intelligence is losing our senses of purpose and direction. We essentially wander aimlessly through life, only to find in middle-age or later that we have wasted many of our years, and that even having a goal for today no longer reduces the enormity of the burdens of our dissatisfactions. Thus, when we do not value or give attention to our very basic needs to increase our social intelligence, our youthful ideals die through their lack of application; when we lose our ideals, we lose our enthusiasm and zest for life.

All in all, when we have low social intelligence, we are much more vulnerable to the devastating effects of unfavorable social conditions and to oppressive exploitation through others' self-centered actions. In addition, we are much more likely to dissipate our limited energies in unproductive ways. When we cannot focus on, or understand, who we are and what we want to do most from our own personal and social perspectives, we lose all possibilities of finding ourselves and of making meaningful contributions to others. We lose our souls through putting on blinders to social realities.

This happens because we cannot build strong identities without a willingness to use our social intelligence for improvement. Our identities govern much of what we do, with the result that this inability to create strong identities rapidly becomes a serious personal and social concern. We are social creatures, conditioned and bonded in some way in each of the most basic areas of society—families, religions and belief systems, the economy, education, and political systems. Unless we are willing to actively acknowledge and honor the deep-seated social roots of our being, we are inevitably cut adrift in the turbulent seas of our complex, chaotic, and ever-widening global society. Severing these basic social connections creates alienating conditions that increase the likelihood that we will become rudderless and lost, without purpose or direction, and therefore essentially destined to lead restricted lives without much hope for reprieve.

IV. The Perils of Having Low Social Intelligence

Loss of Independence

Human beings are interdependent, and we need to know how to balance our dependency needs throughout our lives. When we are young, we do not question our dependency, but rather fight it or carve out ways to grow more independent. When we are more self-sufficient, we exercise some independence, but this is always challenged by our need for attention from other people, and by others' needs to control us in some way. As we go through later life stages, we frequently become dependent once more, and if we are unable to maintain some degree of self-sufficiency, we have to turn to others to help us to survive and thrive.

These ongoing issues about human dependency haunt our personal relationships and our ties with groups, institutions, and society as well as our family bonds. Our need to be as independent as possible is an ideal that has relevance at all stages of our lives, although it is often very difficult to actually achieve this. Rather, other people influence us greatly, and we often allow it because we enjoy the ease with which this happens.

First and foremost, our need to be independent is recognized by, honored, and reflected in our social intelligence. We have to be our own person before we can be anybody, and our actions are not really ours unless we execute them independently. Being responsible requires independence. However, sometimes patterns of deep emotional dependency permeate our lives from generation to generation. When this happens, it may take persistent scrutiny before we know that we are truly independent.

In summation, being independent is a hard-won state of being and doing. We think that we have achieved independence at last, perhaps upon entering a profession, or when we have our first child, but sooner or later we are made painfully aware of our continuing dependency needs, and perhaps of the unwanted extensions of some of our earlier dependency behaviors. It often feels easier to be dependent than to be independent, and the many ways in which we are lured back into some kind of dependency never fail to present themselves as attractive. However, being dependent is a dangerous long-term option, even as we merely go about our daily chores.

Even though our independence is hard-won, it continues to be highly valued by most people. When we speak of fighting to the death to preserve freedom, independence is usually thought of as a vital component of this freedom. We are free only when we think for ourselves, feel for ourselves, and act responsibly. However, this consistency is so often upset that a more generally shared human condition can be thought of as easily being swayed from staying independent at all times.

When we make active use of our social intelligence, it is less difficult to be independent in thought, word, and deed. When we have low social intelligence we may not be truly independent, or we may be in a constant state of losing what little independence we can muster. It is only when we increase our social intelligence that we can have guarantees of increasing our independence.

Using our social intelligence increases the possibilities that we will be able to sustain our independence, even in stressful personal and social times. Although it is easiest of all to lose our independence when we are pressured by others, especially in times of crisis, social intelligence can guide us in placing a higher priority on maintaining our independence in these difficult circumstances. When we are independent we can think more clearly, act more intelligently, and accomplish more.

Having low social intelligence makes it very difficult to distinguish between the different states and degrees of being independent and dependent. When we are not aware of the importance and subtleties of these contrasts, we are less likely to be independent or to desire independence. Furthermore, once we gain some independence, low social intelligence allows us to lose it very easily. Unless we persist in our efforts to increase our social intelligence, we will not be able to win the fight for our own beliefs and principles, and if we lose these we become dangerously dependent on others. We need to think for ourselves rather than to allow others to think for us.

Artificial Roles

A role is a cluster of specific behaviors and social expectations that reflect social standards and goals with respect to the performance of particular tasks or statuses in society. At all stages of the life cycle we are faced with choices of whether or not to play some of the roles with which we are associated according to how others see us in society. For example, the role of boss has shared characteristics whatever the group or organization a particular boss commands. Also, the behavior of young women is influenced by the kinds of opportunities available for women and the range of roles for women in their society. Although we know intellectually that structured role possibilities are human products, or more importantly, social creations, we often do not treat roles as artificial pathways but rather as realities that must be adhered to and respected. There are many real and subtle pressures to conform to role expectations because the solidarity and stability of society depend on things being done in predictable ways.

When we use social intelligence to define our situations, we are more likely to pay close attention to the artificially constructed aspects of roles, and to be critical of their related expectations for us. We then are less likely to conform to others' definitions of roles just for the sake of conforming. Social intelligence brings increased objectivity, as well as some degree of social distance, in our assessments of reality, so that we can see through the vested interests expressed in the social pressures which make us want to merely repeat established patterns of behavior. Social intelligence reduces the perils of becoming trapped or overly enmeshed within roles. This is because SI makes it more likely that we can use our energy to create alternatives to established ways of doing things, thus bringing us closer to the goals and values we really want to realize in our lives.

Modifying role behaviors, and ultimately role expectations, is healthy for individuals and groups because it builds flexibility into the given social structures of society, and it enables more personal goals and objectives to be met, as well as those related to the common good. Although we may gain some degree of security by replaying established traditional roles, we also lose some of our freedoms and the capacity to be authentic. In the long run, and sometimes in the short run, we gain more from distinguishing between who we are as selves and the role behaviors expected of us. If our goal is to increase our life satisfaction, we must get into the habit of being, or trying to become, more real rather than automatically playing a part or a role. This is especially important when we can see from our experiences that we do not gain any valuable benefits from such role-playing.

Roles give conventional signals to individuals and groups, so that even the unknown appears familiar, or at least non-threatening. Roles can be helpful in that they simplify what we think we should do in the sea of complex social realities, but this simplification distorts important aspects of what our social conditions are and who we are. Better to see what is really out there in wider society than to be duped by patterns which limit our options and restrict our potentials and contributions.

When we have low social intelligence, the over-simplification of roles attracts us, and we may easily be drawn into acting in ways that are not in our own long-term interests. Furthermore, role-playing can divert our attention so much that we may put our energy into concentrating on how to impress other people, and whom we should impress, rather than on the nuts and bolts of what we are actually accomplishing through playing certain roles.

We can avoid these particular perils of having low social intelligence by giving our attention to building and increasing our social intelligence. When we do this we become more immune to the negative aspects of role-playing, and we also deliberately choose certain roles to perform when they further our interests or help us to contribute more effectively to the well-being of others. We sometimes gain this level of awareness from experiencing conflicts in our roles. This experience shows us that pain results from solely aiming to please others, or from boredom with repetitive roles. When we actually feel the angst of not acting more decisively in relation to our own ideals, we may become more motivated to increase our social intelligence.

Getting Pushed Around

Some of us fear that if we allow others to dominate us, we will die. This image, in its many variations, becomes the substance of nightmares that replay the essence of our reactions to monsters or bogeymen. Although our real-life situations are, fortunately, rarely as dramatic or sinister as this, there is an element of truth to the idea that we will at least die a slow death if we lose control of who we are. We cannot afford to let others push us around according to their whims, plans, or conspiracies.

A major peril of having low intelligence is that we become more likely to be pushed around by others without even knowing it. We cannot be our own selves when we allow others to direct our behavior in ways which meet those others' needs rather than our own. Furthermore, when we do this we become weaker and more dissatisfied with our lives.

IV. The Perils of Having Low Social Intelligence

Cultivating social intelligence, by contrast, enables us to stay alert to our own interests and goals, and allows us to draw a clearer line to demarcate our own behavior from that of others. When we use our social intelligence we more easily recognize what is really going on in our lives, and we are correspondingly less easily duped by social myths or by what others tell us they are doing. We need to be aware that those who dominate us frequently appear to have the best motives in the world for doing so. For example, husbands may claim to be protecting their wives when they are actually limiting their wives' choices. These husbands' behavior may serve only their own interests in the long run, without taking their wives' well-being into account.

We tend to become victims of being pushed around by others when our social intelligence is blurred by the emotional climate of the milieus in which we interact most frequently. Some of the strongest emotions affecting the clarity of our thinking exist in families, religious settings, work systems, and politics. Dictatorships and genocide have occurred in part because the masses have not known how to use their social intelligence to rebel or resist the dominance of fanatics who have no intention of acting in accordance with a common good.

In order to counteract these perils of low social intelligence, we need to bolster our SI as much as we can at all times. We cannot practice strengthening our social intelligence for only a few hours a week because we will predictably be taken over by the perils of low social intelligence without realizing it. The kind of awareness we must have, if we are to be socially intelligent, is realized every waking hour. We cannot afford to have low social intelligence because the price of our lives is too high to pay.

Sometimes the idea of being our own self at all times is too easily accepted as a truism. Such acceptance is usually only at a superficial level. If we are to be socially intelligent we must experience self in all that we feel, think, and do in order to have a full awareness. Being happy and assuming that everyone is good are usually distorted beliefs that lull us into being overly satisfied with low social intelligence. Similarly, going with the flow can sometimes be more perilous than trying to swim upstream.

Although we consistently benefit from respecting others' opinions, and sometimes from changing some of our behavior to honor others, when we accommodate others too much we dull our social intelligence and add hazards to our daily existence. We do not need to be at war with others, but we cannot often be in perfect or even moderate harmony with them either. Our SI helps us to be more objective about our social realities, so that we do not get off track in unproductive ways. We cannot afford to give others the right to determine what we do for most of the time, which is for most of our lives.

Living on Automatic Drive

When we allow ourselves to live on automatic drive, we cannot act on principle or lead a fully satisfying existence. We move too quickly to be able to maintain a clear awareness of who we are, being propelled largely by others' pressures and expectations. This means that we react habitually to other people and to changing situations in pre-programmed ways, rather than assess circumstances as they evolve.

Living on automatic drive might feel good. We are comforted when we live according to our preconceived ideas, rather than allowing real life to permeate the shield we try to build for ourselves. We do not like to have our beliefs shaken by what happens to us, and we are not inclined to change deeply ingrained patterns of behavior.

When we have low social intelligence we think that we can get by through living automatically. By contrast, thinking is difficult, disconcerting, and brings about the kinds of changes that we want to avoid. However, although living on automatic drive can serve a purpose for many people in the short run—it can help us to get through loss or dramatic upheavals in our personal lives—in the long run we are harmed by not taking ourselves seriously enough to act independently. When we merely react to others, or script all our actions in advance, we cannot fully assess what we should be doing in particular settings.

Therefore, although living on automatic drive can structure our lives and give us some kind of security, these supports will not stand the test of time. In the long run, living on automatic drive leaves us with a sense of having been deceived, of having false experiences. There is no way in which we can be prepared to meet all of life's contingencies by living on automatic drive. The most we can hope for is to have sufficient social intelligence to be able to think on our feet, so that we will land on our feet or be able to get up when all of our supports have been taken away.

IV. The Perils of Having Low Social Intelligence

Living on automatic drive also diminishes the richness of our relationships. We do not want to be automatons, or predictable in our responses. We need to be imaginative and creative if we are to matter to ourselves and to those who are near and dear. Acting according to formula does not help any situation, and it is an ineffective way to deal with social complexities. Social intelligence works with facts and realities rather than searches for ways to evade what is really going on around us.

Living on automatic drive makes us lose our independence, offers us only artificial roles to play in relation to others and to society at large, and makes us vulnerable to others' exploitation. If all we do is react to others, or please them, rather than examine the impact of specific patterns of behavior on us and the common good, we will not be in a position to invest our energies in increasing our social intelligence. We will be so overwhelmed by the continuous series of external demands for our attention that we will not be able to use our energies for more constructive purposes.

Living on automatic drive sets us up for being pushed around by others, and for becoming victims of circumstances rather than social actors. We will not be able to achieve a clear historical sense of what is going on around us when we are caught up in the emotional intensity of our relationships and of our urges to be right or correct. We need flexibility and breathing space in order to be socially intelligent.

Even more detrimental is that living on automatic drive decreases our zest for life. We cannot express ourselves fully if we are geared up for restricted responses to everyday realities. We need to explore the possibilities before us, and we do not have the elasticity we need to do this when we live on automatic drive. Adventures come only to those who are willing to take risks, and when we tether ourselves to our automatic responses we trade what could be for false security.

Decreases Interest

Not having compelling interests to enjoy and express is a serious handicap. When we pursue a career, raise a family, or try to accomplish community change, it is essential that we have the fuel of our interests to move us along toward effective accomplishments. Although there is something intrinsically mysterious about where our interests come from, there are techniques we can develop to help us to keep our interests alive.

One aspect of the mystery of why we have specific interests relates directly to the social conditions of our becoming adults. For example, family processes and the religiosity of significant others may make a big difference in how we experience the world, and in how we explore what matters to us. In this respect, having high social intelligence about who we are and how we act is a guide to knowing what our real interests are.

However, if we have low social intelligence we will have none of the particular interests that would otherwise guide our daily activities in meaningful ways. It is all too easy, with low social intelligence, to be lulled into more or less comfortable states of complacency and apathy. This is eventually experienced as an overriding conviction that our views and behavior do not make any difference to anyone we know, and certainly not to the world at large.

Low social intelligence restricts our options and cramps our potentials through decreasing our interest in our surroundings. When we do not care whether we have satisfactory living or working conditions, we are not about to try to make any changes in these vital aspects of our everyday life. Similarly, when we are not aware of the difference our gender socialization makes in the ways we think and the ways we act, we are not strong enough to formulate goals and objectives that serve our own real interests and the common good. Low SI limits our understanding of the vital roles played by our awareness and our interests in increasing our life satisfaction, and in making the world a better place for more people.

Therefore, low social intelligence dulls our senses and makes us less able to see the broader picture of our lives. When we have low SI, we become listless and entirely lacking in strong passions, especially in the intellectual curiosity necessary for understanding how the world works. Low social intelligence decreases our interests in so many ways that we are left unable to be truly independent, and unable to live fully.

The most effective antidote to the peril of developing a lethal disinterest in the very essence of life is to deliberately create and take initiatives to build our own social intelligence. We always have the possibility of turning the tables of our inclinations, and reversing our tendencies to reduce and diminish our social intelligence. We can call a halt to the extremely destructive momentum of decreasing our interests by making a sufficiently strong commitment to increase our awareness and understanding of what is really going on around us. Cultivating a habit of forcing ourselves to come up with some kind of explanation of our social worlds is one of the most effective starting points for increasing our social intelligence.

It is not accurate to think that people tend to have either high or low social intelligence, but rather that it is important to make the effort to be constantly on the move toward increasing it. We can test our progress through applying SI in the most mundane aspects of our everyday behavior. However, if we fail to make a more or less objective summation of the contexts of our lives, we will be more likely to become victims of the powerful social influences in our relationships and in our broader communities. When we do not make emotional investments in developing and nurturing our own interests, because we have little or no curiosity about how we operate in the world at large, we hasten our essential demise as thinking individuals and responsible agents of change. Only when we have a genuine and deep appreciation of the value of having interests can we begin to pursue what matters most to us. Unless we at least head in this direction, even though we may remain far from achieving real purpose and high social intelligence, our lack of interest will become passivity, and we will gradually abandon our social responsibilities.

A Half-Life

When we greet each other cheerily with the conventional and often meaningless question, "How are you?" we usually want some kind of reading on how the other person is coping with the inevitable hassles of their daily life. Although we may not be ready for the truth underlying a negative response, given the fact that most of us reply affirmatively to this query, we persist in being at least somewhat concerned about our own and others' well-being.

However, when we look closely at the facial expressions of people as they go about their daily business, we see expressions of apparent unrest or boredom, which suggest some shared dissatisfaction in how we conduct our lives. It is rare to see or find individuals who are sufficiently "together" to express a grateful acceptance of whatever is going on in their everyday lives.

This leads to the speculation that having a half-life is not alien to how many of us manage to exist and keep going from day to day. Having a half-life is not exceptional, and although many of us might not readily admit to being only half alive much of the time, there could be more agreement about the idea that many of us are half alive at least some of the time.

In this subdued state, we have low social intelligence. We tune out our surroundings and engage in thoughts and activities that take our minds off our most unpleasant social realities. There are undoubtedly many individual and social benefits from having harmless outlets for some of our inevitable frustrations and conflicts. Our very successful sports and entertainment industries, for example, are built on this premise. In the long run, however, there are many problems and even some severe disadvantages from letting this kind of escape mentality and behavior take over our limited energies.

When we immerse ourselves in our immediate surroundings or activities, we also need to continue to question their place and significance in our broader social contexts. If we do not do this, we may fool ourselves into believing that we are fully alive, because in actual fact we may be retreating from the very real social challenges that should be demanding our close attention. We escape our responsibilities in many different ways, but rather than relieve or strengthen us, this behavior decreases our social intelligence and reduces our options.

However, in some respects we may have to experience being half alive in order to eventually make a serious commitment to live more fully. It is only when we have direct experiences of some of the perils of having low social intelligence that we may become sufficiently motivated to do an about turn and move ourselves out of a cycle of ever-decreasing social intelligence. It is not necessarily destructive, or even disadvantageous, to navigate ourselves through a half-life zone for short periods of time, but it is imperative that we avoid becoming trapped on this track so that we cannot get off and head toward increasing our social intelligence.

In the event that we continue to be half alive through closing down our social awareness, understanding, and options, we will inevitably drift through time and have very little life satisfaction.

IV. The Perils of Having Low Social Intelligence

This is a tremendously high price for us to pay because it inevitably turns into some kind of living death in the long run. We cannot be ourselves and we cannot develop our potentials when we have low social intelligence. The only way out of these perils is to begin to understand more fully who we are and what we want to do in all our social contexts. For example, we need to build our independence and empower ourselves in a variety of social and political situations. We also need to get out of the clutches of others, and to keep our deepest interests alive and well at all times, if we are to meet the real challenges life continues to offer us.

Sources of Social Intelligence

V. Families and Social Intelligence

E ach of us is connected to others through our recurring patterns of interaction, and through the social bonds that are created during these exchanges. However, some interactions are more significant than others with regard to their usefulness in facilitating, developing, and strengthening our social intelligence. For example, our families are the most powerful source of our initial levels of SI; in addition they may continue to define our potentials to increase or decrease our social intelligence, as well as our capacities to deal with the countless challenges and conditions of everyday life.

Patterns in our family relationships are crucial models for all our social interactions whether we realize it or not. Because of the strength of this pivotal influence, our families anchor us as individuals, while at the same time provide us with our finest opportunities to develop effective strategies to increase our social intelligence.

The unique significance of families in large part results from the fact that they are usually the contexts in which we first learn how to negotiate and navigate our ways in the world, especially when we are young and relatively uninfluenced by broader social concerns. It is because of the depth of our emotional roots in our families that we continue to need to interact with our relatives throughout our adult years. We must constantly find new ways to relate to members of our families if we are to mature and be effective in our everyday interactions, and achieve our most meaningful long-range goals.

The value choices we make with respect to our families, as well as the negotiations we conduct within our families, also predispose us toward success or failure in building and applying social intelligence to our most routine decisions and activities. Because our families are the most significant emotional source of our SI, our original and continuing dependencies in our families establish both our limits and possibilities for our behavior. This is so because the emotional dynamics of behavior that occurred when we were young continue to affect us for a lifetime through their tenacity and repetitiveness.

In order to cultivate social intelligence, we must become more objective about our families and the ways in which we behave with respect to them. This increased objectivity allows us to begin to change how we interact with our most significant others, so that ideally we increase our social intelligence and get on with living more effectively. Throughout these processes of coming to see ourselves and our families differently, and of changing how we interact with our relatives, our families are the most challenging arenas we have for testing our emotional strengths, and for making real progress toward reaching our most meaningful goals.

When considering the emotional power that our families wield over us, we need to understand that it is not only our relationships in our immediate families of parents, siblings, and children that have an in-depth impact on our lives. The quality of our exchanges with our extended kin groups also makes a considerable difference to our social intelligence, our behavior, and our life outcomes. For example, the rigidity or flexibility of the bonds of our intergenerational relationships either weakens or strengthens our social intelligence respectively. Furthermore, if we cut ourselves off from our kin groups, or deny their existence, we undermine our possibilities for controlling our lives. By contrast, if we decide to relate as maturely as possible to many different members of our kin groups, we increase our social intelligence, and become more adept at achieving our most cherished goals.

Other characteristics of family relationships can also hurt or support our quests to increase our social intelligence. For example, when our relatives have very tightly knit networks, they inadvertently limit our SI because we cannot get sufficient breathing space to act autonomously. Moreover, it is only if our relatives interact in flexible, open networks that we can participate freely in family events, and at the same time distance ourselves sufficiently from our families in order to engage in broader communities. Thus we increase our social intelligence when we are players in our families, and when we remain anchored in our families as we address broad social concerns through our committed actions.

Family Foundations

The core of our social intelligence derives from the patterns of give-and-take in our families. Even though we may seek to change the nature of the relationship network that produces this core, our families remain crucial influences in how we understand and experience the multiple and complex social influences in our lives. Families are emotional systems, and our social intelligence is built on some of our strongest convictions, as well as on the most basic assumptions we make about ourselves, others, and human nature.

To the extent that self is a product of family interaction, how we see ourselves and the world results from understanding and relating to our families. Furthermore, because our family dependencies may be lethal in their consequences—for example, if we cannot separate ourselves from some important family relationships, we frequently resort to extreme or destructive measures—we need to acknowledge the centrality of their impact on our social intelligence and our life outcomes.

When we think clearly we exercise our social intelligence, which means that we are less likely to become victims of our family dependencies. In other words, when we increase our SI, we strengthen our immunity against the destructive aspects our family relationships can have in our daily lives. Part of this accomplishment rests on our abilities to be objective about ourselves and our families. When we can see our families for what they are, without the rosy lenses of idealism, we are more free to act, and consequently more socially intelligent in our actions.

Our families dictate expectations for a particular division of labor and related caring responsibilities. Although patterns in these expectations vary dramatically across the entire spectrum of society, a common denominator of family labor and family responsibilities is that these influences largely determine our priorities and our investments of energy in daily behavior. Furthermore, it is only by challenging such crucial family expectations that we can strengthen our social intelligence and move into broader social arenas. Although we might decide to conform to our relatives' pressures to behave in certain ways, the deliberateness of our actions will increase our social intelligence. Merely accepting others' definitions, or conforming to others' expectations, diminishes our social intelligence in the long run.

Because family members frequently have strong tendencies to agree on particular standards of behavior, an individual family member must have considerable determination and personal strength to consistently work toward increasing social intelligence. We need to be able to discriminate among our own families' influences on us, so that we may build the foundations of our SI with deliberation. Taking things for granted, and acting in automatic ways, restricts our abilities to develop our social intelligence.

However, when we do manage to act independently, and exercise objectivity in our exchanges with relatives, we often predictably generate family conflicts. It is not easy to increase our social intelligence when family members are pressuring us to behave in ways which further their agendas rather than our own. When we come to discern what is actually in our own best interests, we may have to shake up the family foundations of our social intelligence in order to proceed with our lives more productively.

In many respects these same family foundations provide us with valuable security when we dare to venture into extended social arenas. If we are anchored in our families, we are correspondingly more flexible and versatile in our capacities to move beyond these familiar small group contexts, so that we can make valuable contributions to more people. We also increase our social intelligence when we use our family foundations to launch ourselves into meaningful missions in our communities and in society.

The essence of the power of our family foundations is the forms of emotional bonds that tie us to our relatives. Social intelligence is moved by our passions, and these passions are most clearly expressed in our relationships and interactions with those who are emotionally closest to us. Because our emotions can trap or free us, we have to discover how to choose among them. We are caught up with the emotions that we have learned in our families, and it takes a focused effort and sufficient social intelligence to be able to neutralize these influences.

V. Families and Social Intelligence

Power of Emotions

Above all, social intelligence includes considerable recognition of the power that our individual and collective emotions can wield over us. Many of these influential emotions originate primarily in our families, where we succumb to their power most readily in our tender years. Although the power of emotions can be identified in other social contexts such as religion, our families are the most critical and vital source of how our emotions have been inculcated into our thinking and behavior over the years.

Families express their emotional dynamics in many different ways. For instance, family definitions of right and wrong are necessarily laden with strong positive and negative emotions, bringing with them perceived appropriate sanctions and behavioral responses. We are rewarded or punished when we are children, and in more subtle ways as adults, according to the standards in which our closest relatives believe. Some feelings of right and wrong may be so intense that their consequences are experienced for a lifetime.

Intergenerational connections within our families are another significant aspect of the immense power wielded over us by our families' emotions. Our families are the result of exchanges among many generations of our ancestors. Consequently, the emotional intensity of behavior in past dependencies is shifted down through the different generations, with the result that it tends to be automatically absorbed by today's family members. It is particularly the emotional intensities of past relationships and behavior that are conducted through the generations. We may cope with these pressures well or abysmally, and sometimes these stresses and tensions are so powerful that they entrap members of current generations, or at least strongly inhibit their options.

The strength of specific emotions in families results in part from interpersonal and intergenerational family histories. Emotional power has the potential to overwhelm individuals so completely that they lose their sense of self, and it becomes difficult or impossible for them to exercise social intelligence in relation to this power. However, social intelligence can ultimately temper the more destructive characteristics of powerful family emotions. Increasing social intelligence can be thought of as a worthwhile strategy, sometimes becoming a life-saving endeavor.

It is not necessary to examine, identify, and define specific differences among the powerful emotions in our families as we try to understand why considerable care is needed in order to interact comfortably with our relatives. Rather, it is more socially intelligent, and more effective, merely to observe and make mental notes about the degrees of emotional reactivity which characterize past and present exchanges in our families. We tend to get very involved with some family members rather than others for example. Consequently it may seem to us that the only way to deal with the problematic intensity of being too close to a spouse or a sibling is to cut ourselves off from that relationship. Divorce is generally a legal resource that helps us to break away from our problematic closeness with our spouses. Similarly, increased emotional distance or geographical separation becomes a way to regulate relationships between siblings who are over-involved with each other. In both situations, the extreme reactivity of spouses and siblings is reduced by these makeshift strategies.

Social intelligence offers us a different way to resolve the pain of losing our identities in these kinds of overly close family relationships. When we are socially intelligent, we understand that there are constructive ways to separate ourselves emotionally from our significant others. If we are able to do this, we are not emotionally obliged to rupture close relationships or remove ourselves from them.

Gaining objectivity about the emotional power that runs throughout our family bonds is an essential first step in using our social intelligence to control our reactivity to other family members. As we pull out emotionally from our most demanding or draining family bonds, we can begin to think about how we want to interact in these relationships, rather than be compelled to react to them. We are socially intelligent when we recognize the power of emotions in how our families function, face the emotional facts of our families for what they are, reduce cycles of reactivity and predictability in our nuclear and kin relationships, and work toward attaining our most meaningful family freedoms.

Family Freedoms

One of the most important principles of social intelligence is that most of us benefit not from leaving our families in order to be free, but from claiming our freedom or autonomy through and in relation to our families. Knowing our families well, and realizing their power to influence and limit our choices, is an essential precondition for finding and exercising these family freedoms.

Being human includes being driven by deep-seated social needs to belong to at least a few groups. The fact that our families are frequently the only meaningful groups with which we interact from cradle to grave means that they are supremely significant arenas in which we can increase and exercise our social intelligence. We can think of ourselves as ultimately being participants in streams or torrents of intergenerational connections, with this location or source being either an anchor of security, or an overwhelming force that does not consistently respond to our real interests. At worst, we run the risk of being annihilated by the power that intergenerational emotions can wield over us.

Family freedoms come in many different shapes and sizes. They may be thought of as seemingly minuscule aspects of family interaction, such as individual decisions to attend family gatherings, and at the same time as major forays into communities and broad social arenas such as special interest international organizations. We are historical beings as well as social actors; the spectrum of possibilities that flows from these aspects of our human relatedness is governed by the kind or degree of social intelligence which we cultivate and exercise during our day-to-day activities. Similarly the freedoms we take, and the effectiveness of our contributions to families, communities, and society demonstrate the strength of our social intelligence.

Being able to exercise our autonomy within our families suggests that we have some control over how we handle the power of our family emotions. If we are caught up in well-established ruts of individual and family reactivity, we cannot think clearly or recognize the social context and connections that characterize our everyday behavior. When we succumb to the power of family emotions in this way, we diminish our social intelligence through reacting to others rather than thinking through how we really want to relate to them.

By contrast, when we are sufficiently independent in using our social intelligence to orient and guide our behavior, we can maintain our family responsibilities, let go of the destructive aspects of our family relatedness, and launch ourselves more effectively into society at large. Consequently, our most precious family freedom is to be able to live successfully in both of the social worlds of our kin connections and the global community. When we accomplish this we can be both here and there, at least symbolically, through managing to keep our two worlds in a state of creative tension with each other. In this respect, our personal family life informs the more goal-directed roles we choose to assume in society and vice versa. Our social intelligence results from and is influenced by our awareness of these kinds of small and large group connections in our lives, and by our willingness and talents to act responsibly in both arenas.

Because our behavior influences the quality and degree of our social intelligence, we safeguard our well-being when we act thoughtfully in both near and far domains. We increase our SI by deliberately subjecting ourselves to the multiple social challenges we are faced with when we participate as fully as possible in both personal and societal arenas. In the long run we thrive from these varied real-life opportunities to experience and understand more of the complexities of society. However, at the start of such an endeavor, in the short run, this kind of dual participation may create painful stress. At its best, social intelligence gives us the capacity to come up with effective yet measured ways for involvement with others. Socially intelligent involvement means that we do not have to pay the unwelcome and unhealthy price of becoming pawns in relation to the push and pull of those who do not have our best interests at heart.

Traps and Hazards

Common sense, which is a shared, conventional way of thinking, suggests that it is usually wise for us to fit in with our families and do what is expected of us. By contrast, social intelligence, being more firmly based on facts and knowledge than common sense, encourages us to challenge the authority of our family elders or peers, and to orient our behavior according to our own most cherished goals, rather than to those of other family members. Cultivating social intelligence enables us to avoid the traps and hazards of going along with family expectations, and guides us toward identifying our real choices and being more in charge of our decisions.

V. Families and Social Intelligence

Some of the traps that await us in our families, particularly when our thinking is befuddled by wanting to please others, include believing that those who are emotionally closest to us understand us, and being willing to follow relatives' directions and suggestions uncritically. We need to realize that once we move toward achieving that which is not truly of our own choosing, we can waste decades of our limited lives by trying to deal with others' standards and pressures.

Additional traps include being sabotaged by needy family members, who are likely to have their own interests at heart rather than ours. Whatever we do, there will be constant pulls for our attention and assistance from those relatives who are most dependent on us. Part of what makes these kinds of traps so pernicious is that we are often naively full of good will, or the desire to help, so that we end up being unable to help ourselves in light of these particular emotional pressures.

When we have strong social intelligence we can see who we are in a more objective and realistic perspective. We are better grounded in ourselves and in our own goals, and consequently less likely to be dislodged by others' requests, even from our most beloved family members. SI grants us a healthy degree of immunity to the emotional push and pull of our families. It protects us and makes our interactions in broad social arenas increasingly effective, without at the same time allowing our goals to replace or undermine our family responsibilities to respond to others' needs.

Besides these major family traps, which can ensnare us, there are other, more subtle hazards which sap our emotional strength and energy. For example, we frequently try too hard to live up to conventional standards of being a good spouse or a good parent. In the long run, many traditional roles are not effective or reliable guides for everyday behavior. The given complexity of social realities makes it necessary for each one of us to deliberately forge, for ourselves, what it means to be a good person who has specific family responsibilities. We must not allow ourselves to be duped by particular role models, or by what others do, if we are to be guided by social intelligence in our efforts to live with a greater degree of authenticity.

Other family hazards include the tendency to repeat decisions and life choices that our relatives and ancestors have made before us, without being really sure that this is what we want to do. In the past, most young adults followed in the footsteps of their parents. Even though in today's society education enables individuals to make quantum leaps in their achievements and goals in comparison to previous generations of the same family, a strong emotional current of connection still makes relatives' past behavior, at the very least, a fall-back option. This pattern of imitation needs to be tested by our experiences, however, and assessed by our social intelligence, before we allow ourselves to be sufficiently tempted to follow in another family member's footsteps.

Both traps and hazards exist because we continue to be vulnerable to our families in spite of our more advanced education and increased career options. We continue to be dependent on this group of significant others, at least to some extent, as we grow and mature, and even in old age we need to recognize the many family challenges that face us if we are to live fully. However, this condition of being continuously subjected to the traps and hazards of our families does not mean that we should have nothing to do with our families. Rather it is wisest, and most socially intelligent, if we deliberately stay involved with our families. To the extent that we interact with as many family members as possible, at the same time making sure that we use our SI in our exchanges with our relatives, we will correspondingly be more protected from family traps and hazards.

It is only through changing the ways in which we relate to our families that we can become more socially intelligent, and consequently more able to avoid or deal with family traps and hazards. On the other hand, if we cut ourselves off from our relatives in order not to subject ourselves to their negative influences, we will be more likely to be completely overtaken by unexpected traps and hazards. These traps and hazards have links to our families, but they may manifest themselves in other social contexts. For example, we need to overcome deep-seated sibling rivalry within our families if we are to be able to resolve the traps and hazards of competition in work or political situations.

Challenges to Social Intelligence

One reliable sign that we have increased our social intelligence while interacting with our families is that sooner or later we need to deal with negative reactions and pressures from our relatives. In fact it is only as we increase our social intelligence, continue to grow, and become increasingly independent that negative reactions and pressures from our relatives are predictably evoked.

The kinds of changes that tend to flow from increasing our social intelligence may create marked shifts in our usual patterns of behavior within our families, with the inevitable consequence that our relatives will gradually exert pressure on us to go back to being our more accommodating selves. However, when we make a habit of exercising SI in our exchanges with our families, it gradually becomes apparent— and more acceptable—to our relatives that we do not place behaving according to their wishes and expectations for us high among our new priorities.

Social intelligence helps us to be aware of and ready for these changes and their aftermath, and to cope effectively with this fallout. For example, if being more socially intelligent in our postures and exchanges with our relatives is distinctively different from how we used to behave, our families' reactions may be very negative. Furthermore, when our new patterns of behavior are a dramatic contrast to how we used to behave, some of our most emotionally significant relatives may even threaten withdrawal from their relationships with us. Thus the more different from our former selves we become by cultivating and strengthening our social intelligence, the greater our families' tendencies will be to try to manipulate us so that we give up our newfound ways.

The inevitability of this chain of events and the difficulty of firmly standing our own ground—given opposition and resistance from those who are nearest and dearest to us—may make increasing our social intelligence so daunting that we decide to give up trying to become more socially intelligent. However, the intensity of our families' reactions to the unfolding of our more aware selves—a promising and even a sure sign that our new behavior is effective—diminishes through time if we commit ourselves to sustaining our efforts to be socially intelligent in spite of familial opposition.

Several strategies can help us to weaken the intensity of our family members' discomfort with our increased social intelligence, and hence their resistance to the changes introduced by our increased SI. One reliable strategy is for us to deliberately stay emotionally close to our relatives at the same time that we carve out new lives for ourselves. If we interact with as many family members as possible at the same time that we try to establish new ways of relating to them, the emotional reactivity of our families gradually settles down and becomes positively affected by our persistent efforts to be more socially intelligent.

In assessing the advantages and disadvantages of this kind of damage control while interacting with our families, some of the advantages of increasing our social intelligence through family exchanges need to be reconsidered. The main reason for increasing our social intelligence through interacting with our families is that these emotionally significant others give us the most real and difficult challenges we can have with regard to who we are and how socially intelligent we are. In order to be more socially intelligent we need to exercise or test our social intelligence in family contexts that will not disappear overnight. However much our relatives may disagree with the changes we introduce since becoming more socially intelligent, we cannot as easily be abandoned in these efforts by our families as by other individuals or groups. In other words, we need the emotional toughness and tenacity of our families to respond to us in order to be sure that we are growing and maturing through increasing our social intelligence.

Change in the Long Run

Social intelligence suggests that we need to know how to maintain change in the long run if we are to accomplish the personal and collective goals in which we believe the most. It is of no avail to have short-term gains if, over time, we get lost in the complex push and pull of our daily lives, or if we lose sight of our higher ideals, goals, and priorities. We neutralize or even negate all our efforts when we cannot sustain our early enthusiasms for action in order to accomplish the tasks immediately at hand, or when we get distracted and diverted from our most important objectives.

Given this individual and social reality, we must ask ourselves what we need to do if we are to proceed with making the kinds of changes we want to make in the long haul. First, it is important to think of some of these changes in relation to our

70

family dependencies, thus necessitating an ongoing series of more enlightened exchanges with our relatives. It is essential that we learn to maintain a stand for ourselves and our deepest convictions within our families, and this task is thoroughly accomplished when we interact continuously with those who are emotionally closest to us.

Having ongoing family dependencies does not mean that our relatives tolerate us the best, or support us the most. Rather, our families present us with our strongest challenges, and we grow best when we have to muster the stamina or emotional competence to deal with family conflicts, family pressures to conform, and disinterest from those relatives we care about the most. Although there are many times when our families support us, this usually happens for functional short-term purposes, or when our personal and family agendas happen to overlap. All other things being equal, our families at least initially resist many of our more independent accomplishments because our changed behavior destabilizes the family status quo, or threatens our individual family relationships.

One example of the kind of independence that families resist is a family member's decision to live in a different or distant geographical area. Another example is a family member's plan to follow a career, such as acting, which may be remote from the experiences of most members in a particular family. More obvious instances of family opposition to independence include situations where a proposed marriage partner is perceived as not meeting familial standards and expectations, and shifts in relationships that occur when a family member switches political or religious affiliations.

In these examples of individuals' changes, which tend to be long-lasting, relatives may band together to try to reverse their family members' wishes to change their status, or they may find more subtle ways to sabotage that family member's pursuit of independence. In any event, it takes social and emotional fortitude to go ahead with unpopular moves, and individuals wanting to make changes risk creating temporary rifts and schisms in their families.

Some of the optimal social conditions for making long-term changes in our family relationships, which frequently result from increasing SI, come into being when individuals making the changes also deliberately stay in meaningful contact with their relatives. It appears that we may need the stimulus of implementing our preferred goals in a creative tension with the resistance of our most significant others, especially if we are to be successful in ultimately achieving our goals. Furthermore, even when our objectives are accomplished, we maintain our changed statuses through both continuing to cultivate social intelligence and maintaining the kind of independence that allows us to meet our ongoing family responsibilities.

Our families give us the emotional security of lifelong commitments that are always in the making. Although we may convince ourselves that we can get along without family connections, such life patterns will eventually show less social intelligence and diminished motivation to contribute to the common good. We need to maintain balance in our original family relationships, without being overwhelmed or dominated by them, so that we can think more clearly in all social settings, and act according to our own socially intelligent priorities. If we are emotional refugees from our own families, we easily become victims of other emotional and social systems, such as competitive work groups or religious cults. We cannot afford to sacrifice the richness and security of our lifelong family connections, especially since our families have the quality of being an enduring influence in our social arenas and in our innermost lives.

VI. Religion and Social Intelligence

R eligions are established, legitimate sources of wisdom. Their tenets are usually time tested, and their specific beliefs offer great solace and hope because they deal directly with concerns about everyday problems, our deepest fears, and life after death.

Our early ancestors lived mostly in magical rather than religious worlds, which helped them to adapt to their particularly harsh living conditions. Even though today magic tends to be associated with the occult, or with sophisticated manipulations like advertising in modern industrial societies, we still have a relatively strong sense of awe and mystery about ourselves and the world about us. Evolution, education, and social development have not led us to abandon religious or magical beliefs and practices. Rather, our more developed brains, our learning, and our social complexity provide us with increased opportunities to honor traditional and modern religious beliefs, as well as to express new ideas and experiences as sacred and secular beliefs.

Because of this invaluable social heritage of religion and magic, both religious and secular beliefs are significant sources of social intelligence. Religions and other belief systems sustain many of our most significant values and attitudes about who we are and who others are. Furthermore, because religions draw upon beliefs in supernatural powers, religion is often more compelling as a social influence on our behavior than other aspects of society. However, the impact religion has on us ultimately depends on whether an individual or a group views a particular religion as salient and meaningful.

Our beliefs, and what we think are the origins of our beliefs, are important because they motivate our behavior. In many respects we are who we believe we are, whatever the facts of our particular situations. Furthermore, religions suggest, or even dictate, crucial definitions and assumptions we make about self and others. For example, according to some religions, human beings are all flawed because of our shared condition of original sin; we must love our neighbors as ourselves if we are to be worthy; or hard work and material gain are moral duties.

Social intelligence is useful because it helps us to be more objective about our religious and secular beliefs; it increases our freedom to assess our existing beliefs for what they are. SI can also guide us to develop new religious beliefs within the same religious tradition or in other religious, spiritual, or social spheres. Increasing our social intelligence may increase or decrease our religiosity because SI strengthens our capacities to move beyond our specific fears or apprehensions about taking action. In this respect, social intelligence helps us to benefit from our beliefs, rather than allows our beliefs to inhibit our plans and strategies to change ourselves or to increase the common good.

Although religious communities usually encourage their true believers to accept all the beliefs of a particular religion, this is frequently difficult to do, or impractical, given individuals' different levels of maturity and responsibility. Social intelligence increases our capacities to make decisions about which religious beliefs we will cherish most, and which religious traditions we will question.

One result of this process of refining and decreasing or extending our religious beliefs according to the principles of social intelligence is that we may become more peripheral in relation to an established religious denomination. However, at the same time that this happens, our private and public observances and devotions in this same religious tradition may become more meaningful and influential in our daily lives. We benefit from being able to articulate our most cherished beliefs and principles, so that we can live more clearly according to them, rather than merely conform to religious rituals in the hope that some day they will become more meaningful to us. Using our social intelligence to better understand the substance of differences between traditional and non-traditional sources of wisdom highlights our options, and helps us to better navigate ourselves and negotiate with others in a rapidly changing world.

VI. Religion and Social Intelligence

Even though an individual may find that traditional religious beliefs are not relevant to present day social realities or personal identity, such beliefs can be one of our most meaningful and influential starting points for the development and practice of social intelligence. Religious values give us a world view, sanctify different aspects of our everyday behavior, and serve as a lifelong challenge to our more mundane beliefs, doubts, and practices.

Religion and Everyday Beliefs

Our individual and collective beliefs are a powerful influence in our lives. Even though we might say that some religions, such as Judaism, emphasize that our actions are more important and powerful than our beliefs, it is our beliefs in action, or in the value of specific actions, which consistently move us to do what we do. In brief, we have to believe in the supreme importance of action in order to make action a priority in our lives as a whole.

From the point of view of social intelligence, our beliefs set up a series of assumptions about self and others, which then enable us to define reality. Our beliefs also guide us to act, or not to act, in the situations we find ourselves in. Ideally, we choose which beliefs we want to nurture, so that we can increase the control we have over our behavior and its outcomes.

Religions can be defined as clusters of beliefs, principles, doctrines, or dogmas. Each religion has its own literature of wisdom that shows which of its beliefs are the most sacred and essential to that religion. Most religious beliefs address the central significance of our relationships to a supernatural being, such as God, and the quality of our personal bonds with others. The secular tool of social intelligence provides us with many different ways to consider and assess more closely the impact of our religious beliefs on the decisions we make, and on the ways we allow our religions to define what we do.

Another property of our religious beliefs is that they can influence most or all of our everyday beliefs. However, if religion is not an important aspect of our lives, we will necessarily have to build a series of secular beliefs to help us to understand the many situations we find ourselves in. We need either sacred or secular beliefs to make sense of our lives, and to act as springboards of motivation for our actions and contributions to society.

Social Intelligence in Everyday Life

One of the ways in which we can compare and contrast religious and secular beliefs is to examine, through using our social intelligence, the impact that particular beliefs have on our day-to-day behavior. A belief in original sin, for example, may prevent us from exercising our own initiatives, and from respecting and acting upon our own ideas. In contrast to many religious beliefs, secular beliefs can be politically empowering, and may inspire individuals and groups to act on behalf of historically momentous social causes such as human rights. In this instance people's motivations to act are clearly increased by their secular beliefs and principles, such as the importance of social equality and justice for all.

Everyday beliefs can also be thought of more broadly, that is, to include all the beliefs we have about us and other people. Often we do not think that what we believe about who we are—or what we believe about those with whom we interact on a daily basis—has an impact on what we do. However, social intelligence shows us that in essence and deed people are very much a product of the different kinds of beliefs that they entertain. For example, if we believe that we are a gentleman or a lady, we might find that our deeply ingrained civilized niceties do not stand us in good stead for dealing effectively with the cutthroat competitiveness characterizing the business world.

Social intelligence helps us to separate beliefs that enable us to be productive human beings from beliefs that limit our participation in the world. Although some religious beliefs severely restrict what we are willing to do, other religious beliefs can be extremely valuable in that they add persistence to our efforts in community projects. We may believe, for example, that we are truly doing God's will as we consistently work for the betterment of others. Furthermore, the sanctity of this kind of religious commitment may carry us forward in our endeavors for a lifetime, rather than merely for a few months or years. We learn, and social intelligence shows us, that we can transcend many harsh social realities when we have deep religious beliefs, especially when we deliberately exercise those beliefs in our daily actions.

Defining Social Reality

When we use our social intelligence, we quickly realize the strength of the historical and contemporary influences that religion and other belief systems, such as science, have in formulating our world views, in deepening our understanding of self and others, and in making assumptions about what is socially significant in our everyday lives. Religious perspectives are particularly powerful because they highlight what is believed to be sacred, or of supreme importance in our complex social realities, and they suggest what is to be deemed harmful, pernicious, or evil. Religions often define right and wrong for many people, and whether we ourselves are true believers or not, religious maxims bring their weight to bear in many personal, social, and cultural settings.

In using our social intelligence, we can begin to assess more critically the importance and personal significance of both our sacred and secular beliefs. For example, with the help of SI, we may decide to believe a particular religion in a totalistic way, or we may choose to be more selective in ordering the specific priorities of that religion. Social intelligence challenges us to scrutinize our religious and secular beliefs more rationally, especially those beliefs that may be thought of as part of our blind faith.

However, at the same time that we undertake a close examination of our most fundamental values, social intelligence also helps us to acknowledge a deep human thirst and hunger for meaning. Religious belief, for example, has the power to transcend routine drudgery and banal circumstances in our day-to-day lives. One of the most significant factors in our socially intelligent awareness of religions' influences on our daily lives is the knowledge that we have the capacity to choose what we should or must do. Social intelligence and religions enable us to decide which religious beliefs we want to subject ourselves to, and to which religious beliefs we can commit ourselves.

In some respects, certain religious dimensions may be indispensable to our successful cultivation of social intelligence. Historically religions have offered us early but meaningful explanations of the universe, which may or may not have been supported during a society's development of secular knowledge. There is some agreement among social scientists, for example, that religions have helped human beings to adapt to harsh, static, or rapidly changing environments, and that religious commandments have successfully guided countless generations toward establishing some kind of viable moral order in society. In fact, even from a contemporary viewpoint, it seems that many religions continue to have meaningful answers for difficult human and social problems that science cannot yet address, and that these ideas can be incorporated as a particular form of wisdom within our social intelligence.

Whenever we seek to understand or change our life situations, we are compelled to return to what we take for granted about our relationships to other people, or about our assessments of our social circumstances. It is at this level that religion can lead us toward hope, inspiration, or prophecy in facing the unknown.

Even the experience of despair can become a constructive step toward increasing our social intelligence. When we know who or what the enemies are that threaten to dissipate our purpose, direction, and satisfaction, we can deal with our social realities more capably. Religion helps us to sort out those aspects of our lives that are more desirable and should be kept, or those that are feared and therefore should be discarded. We can make reliable assessments of what we want or do not want more easily and effectively when we make comparisons with some of our most cherished religious or ethical ideals.

Contemporary trends in new religious movements of spirituality make deliberate efforts to keep the essence of wisdom within religions alive and well in our daily exchanges. For example, we can use religious beliefs to enable us to see more clearly how we can be fulfilled in the present, particularly through addressing the social realities of our families and communities, rather than by merely repeating particular rituals or formal religious ceremonies. Social intelligence is enriched by incorporating some of religion's basic organizing principles, particularly because they play a crucial and central role in defining and understanding existing social realities, and in creating more beneficial social realities.

Sanctification

Because contemporary denominational religions worship one God, they suggest an ordering of values and virtues that are supposed to help us to draw closer to the Almighty. Some beliefs and codes of conducts are considered to be more spiritual or holy than others. When we learn and practice these principles within particular religions, we can choose to become more worthy of God in what we think and do.

Being religious includes this kind of sanctification of our lives. When we dedicate ourselves to particular religious beliefs or actions, each aspect of our daily lives becomes a spiritual

78

experience. Some of the most highly motivated leaders in history believed that they had a calling, or a religious vocation. Social intelligence enhances this experience because it allows us to be more aware of these processes, and to take a more active part in choosing what we will sanctify through our thoughts, behavior, practices, and communities.

One of the advantages of social intelligence is that we can be more objective about matters of the heart, including our religious beliefs. SI reduces the soporific characteristics of religion, which can easily lull us into a complacent passivity. By contrast, when we use our social intelligence, we keep alert and awake, and monitor what we do according to the values we really believe in or want to espouse. This means that as we increase our SI, we also expand our capacities to be enlightened, which may be similar to religious experience.

When we use our social intelligence, we do not have to accept what others believe totally or uncritically, even when these beliefs are integral parts of traditional religious or faith systems. However, at the same time, it makes us more respectful of beliefs that have had lasting power throughout history or many generations in our own families. When we are socially intelligent, we may choose to be religious in orthodox ways, or reject conventional religious beliefs. SI helps us to be acutely aware of belief systems and their diverse influences on our lives, and this awareness at the same time enables us to be more immune to the harmful effects of religion. We are less likely to become victims of others' beliefs when we count on our own abilities to discern and choose those religious values that will sanctify our lives.

In these respects, the deliberate sanctification of our daily routines does not replicate a particular religious community's dictates. We decide which religious values we want to cherish most, so that they become the most sacred part of our lives. When we sanctify that which is most important to us, we act in enlightened ways. We take control of our yearning for religious experience by establishing purpose, meaning, and direction as ways to sanctify our actions.

In its broadest sense, therefore, sanctification is not merely a way to be religious or spiritual. We increase meaning in what we do when we establish our own priorities, such as defining ways in which we can acknowledge and celebrate our own understanding of sacred times or places. Even though our sense of sacred times and places could well duplicate traditional belief systems, when we are socially intelligent, we may choose to modify conventional patterns of religious observance and practices. True believers criticize such variations, or label them as irreligious, sinful, deviant, or heretical, but SI helps us not to be insulted, especially when we understand that this reaction is often insular ignorance, a lack of appreciation of diversity, or resistance to change.

In many respects, sanctification increases our health and vitality. When we allow our social intelligence to guide us in all matters, including religion, we enjoy a deeper peace of mind about who we are, our relationships, and our communities, and we are better able to live with true commitment to the common good. Social intelligence keeps our spiritual core alive and well, and we are stronger and more able to give of ourselves to others.

Sanctification of an individual's private and public everyday life is a preliminary step in making communities and society more sacred. Sanctifying who we are and what we do gives us a stronger vision of what things could be in the world around us. This optimism allows us to have more empathy for others, and we celebrate diversity more willingly when we honor our own specific value choices. The more we observe our sacred times and places in our various daily routines, the more our behavior will be unencumbered by negative diversions and activities. Exercising individual responsibility to sanctify our behavior means that we elevate ourselves to higher planes of appreciation, respect, and contributions to others.

False Idols

Many western religions warn us, and at the same time command us, not to worship anything or anybody other than the one true God of their belief systems. One of the applications of this principle of religious or spiritual wisdom is that whenever we concentrate our efforts in a particular direction, making these activities of supreme importance in our daily activities, we need to ask ourselves what or who it is we are worshiping in this way. Upon reflection, if we really believe that we are responding to a holy vocation, or to our understanding of what God's will is for us, our behavior could well be thought of as moving us and others toward the glorification of one God. However, if on the other hand, we find that we are largely driven by our own materialistic ambitions to achieve great financial successes, we may well be worshipping false idols through our actions.

In brief, when we allow false idols to dominate our lives, we diminish our capacities to give appropriate attention to the importance of the common good and social justice. From well-established religious perspectives, God may be understood as being justice in process; therefore, by extension, the contributions we make that reduce social inequities can be thought of as holy or sanctified in that they are efforts to do God's work. By contrast, being obsessed with selfish gains shows how false idols can get us off a path which would lead us to make beneficial changes in society. The worship of materialism, for example, means that we get so wrapped up in narrowly defined, selfish goals that we lose sight of the greater good.

Religions ground us in the important moral and social principle of avoiding the worship of false idols. When we are socially intelligent, we are better able to discern the significance of broad social needs together with our own responsibilities to address these needs. Social intelligence also makes us more likely to respect and make use of the moral support of religions in addressing these concerns, as well as to value consistency in formulating attainable goals that increase social justice in society.

These constructive ideals are bolstered by what may appear to be negative beliefs about false idols. When we have an increased understanding of some of the ultimately destructive consequences of spending our limited human energies and resources in paying homage to false idols, we obtain greater clarity about what it takes to concentrate our actions on doing God's will.

Social intelligence, like other aspects of individual and collective human endeavor, can be abused as a false idol. When we use social intelligence only for private gain, or even for the destruction of others, we make it into a false idol. However, when we use it to further an enlightened agenda of bringing about constructive change in the lives of less advantaged people, this objective becomes congruent with the worship of one true God.

One of the tests for which direction we are going in is to examine our bodies' responses to our behavior, and the responses of those who are directly affected by our actions. If we are strong and sufficiently able to give of that strength to meet others' needs, it is more likely that our acts are in line with furthering the social ideals of the conventional religions of our times, which spell out human beings' responsibilities to the supreme moral or ethical power in the universe. Furthermore, we are able to discern the fruit of our actions if we are worshipping one true God through making social contributions. By contrast, serious individual and social problems frequently follow in the wake of behavior that is focused solely on false idols.

Therefore, in order to increase our social intelligence, we need to distinguish among those of our acts that have positive or productive individual and social consequences, and those that do not. In this respect, the moral codes of established religions can be thought of as guides for achieving those principles of social intelligence that keep us relatively immune from the allure and negative demands of false idols.

Commitments

Having religious faith can be thought of as a manifestation of our personal and social commitments. A more specific example of this idea is that when we say that our values derive from a particular religion, we suggest that we are committed to principles shared by believers in the same religious tradition. Individuals who make these kinds of commitments to religious beliefs try to elevate their daily behavior to expressing praise for God. Furthermore, their deep-seated assent to particular religious teachings frequently makes their actions persistent and unwavering in their objectives, and ultimately hallmarks of their productive commitments.

We may also make strong commitments to individuals or groups of people. For example, we sanctify our bonds to our spouses and children when we honor our commitments to them. We tend to be loyal and faithful to those we care for most because of the emotional commitments we make to them.

We also make commitments to a course of action. When we establish life-long goals to pursue, and remain true to our efforts to achieve them come what may, we follow paths of commitment and faith. Our commitments give us the strength to persist in our accomplishments, sometimes in spite of numerous setbacks and heartbreak.

VI. Religion and Social Intelligence

Social intelligence gives us a new view of the commitments we make in our lives, and the ways in which our commitments can move us forward. We are more productive and respected when we can make and keep commitments to others. When we are committed believers in a particular religious tradition, it is usually easier for us to face failure or hardship if our commitments to people, places, or things do not turn out as we had hoped.

Social intelligence also helps us to understand why carrying out our commitments frequently increases our well-being. When we are immature or in great pain, the easiest thing for us to do is to break off a troublesome commitment and make a fresh start in a different social setting. However, when we exercise emotional fortitude, we are able to transcend our automatic reactions and strong inclinations to flee the scene, and instead continue to work at maintaining or re-forging our commitments. SI shows us that a critical aspect of human behavior, one that distinguishes people from animals, is the very important capacity to make and maintain commitments.

When we consider the span of history we can see that religions are often reliable sources for principles worthy of individual and collective commitment. We are more comfortable making personal commitments to those who share the same or similar religious beliefs because religion is a body of wisdom that has been tested through time and in many difficult circumstances. This impressive heritage of religions often makes us feel strongly that we can truly depend on religious sources, at least until our own experiences prove them wrong. Religious principles have been used successfully for many generations, and although social intelligence enables us to appreciate how religion can also exploit and oppress people, in the long run religious truths and their believers may represent a powerful and dependable social influence for good.

One of the major characteristics of commitment, from the point of view of social intelligence, is that committed action is frequently, if not characteristically, non-rational or unreasonable. We sometimes stick with beliefs, family members, friends, projects, and ways of being that defy the odds, or even contradict our own interests. Although this lack of rationality may suggest that from time to time it is best for us to break some of our commitments, on the whole we do not usually allow any lack of reason to dissuade us from honoring our commitments. In fact, we may become more committed with regard to the essential good of our commitments when all the evidence before us points in the other direction.

Commitments are very powerful individual and social influences in our everyday lives. We are who we are, and we do what we do in large part because of the commitments we have made or will make. Making commitments helps to immunize us against the vagaries of our conditions and situations, and we feel stronger and more in charge of our decision-making when we deliberately forge commitments which are the most meaningful to us.

Religion and Identity

Religion is sometimes the bedrock of our beliefs, values, ideals, and principles, and may therefore be a primary source for creating personal and social identities. We frequently use the label of a particular religion, for example, to describe the most important beliefs we espouse, and the kinds of actions and activities that we revere most. However, this form of social identity may be close or distant from our personal identity, which is who we really are in our day-to-day activities.

When we decide to identify with a religion, we automatically buy into a basic set of assumptions about reality, as well as a series of specific ways to define and simplify the many complex situations in which we find ourselves. Because religion is a reliable source of values, it frequently sheds light on significant aspects of our shared social condition. It is because of this universal characteristic of religious belief systems that many individuals choose to identify themselves through a religious denomination. Although it may be less common to cling to social identities that originate in particular religions in modern industrial societies, religious social identities have worn well. They have survived so many harsh social realities that they continue to be valuable sources of sustenance today, especially in less developed societies.

Social intelligence shows us the type of emotional and ethical strength we can receive from traditional religious identities. SI also makes us aware that one size does not fit all, and that we are inevitably challenged by circumstances to carve out more individualistic, personal identities in relation to our deepest religious beliefs and priorities. Because we have deep-seated needs to explain the mysterious or the impossible that we observe in society and in our relationships, we turn to more individualized approaches to religion. Similarly, when we cannot readily find meaning in the immediate terms of our everyday existence, it is comforting to turn to religious sources for inspiration and motivation.

One consequence of seeking to understand our lives in relation to basic religious ideas is that these ideas can empower us. This end product may be deliberately sought or accidental. When we believe we have a purpose or a mission in life, or when we believe we are born for a reason, have a religious vocation, or a deep-seated sense of meaning according to a particular belief system, we are stronger than if we do not have these beliefs. Thus religion can enhance our everyday experiences, so that we are able to transcend our personal selfishness and work for the good of all.

In many respects, the more personal identity that we can build from religion stands us in better stead than a complete social identification with the traditions and beliefs of a particular religion. If our social identities are ready-made in this way, we do not learn as much or grow as much from questioning and finding out which religious values and beliefs dominate us, or that we want to govern the course of our actions.

It is much easier for most of us to create an artificial social identity with religion than it is to create a false personal identity. At an individual level each person tends to assess what a particular belief means, while at a social level all the beliefs of a particular religion may be accepted unconditionally, that is, without really understanding what they imply for that person's everyday behavior.

Building identity through making deliberate value choices about religious beliefs develops both spirituality and social intelligence. When we heighten our awareness of the relationship between religious principles and ethical concerns, for example, we can use religious values as a perspective and a guide for our decision-making in all aspects of our being and doing. Also, at the same time that we cultivate our individual identities and social intelligence, we have the strength to withstand the complex and powerful pressures of social life, to hold our own with respect to others' views, and to achieve our most cherished goals. In these ways religion has many secular effects on our behavior, and what we believe—especially about our identities and who we are—influences what we do in any given situation.

VII. Social Class and Social Intelligence

Though we may not wish it to be so, or even may not be aware of it, we all belong to social classes of some kind. Whether we think of social class as a grouping, which is based on economic assets, or as a gender group, race, ethnic group, or religion, we, and others, are perceived as being members of these classes. Because of the complexity of such social identifications, our social class memberships frequently overlap, and we end up being members of several social classes at the same time.

Social intelligence takes this important fact of social life into account when it helps us to assess any given situation, or when it guides our search for a deeper understanding of the usual social conditions of our daily lives. We are who we are and we do what we do in many respects because of the social class placements we claim for ourselves, or those that are bestowed upon us, frequently by others who are more powerful.

Social classes are important to recognize and deal with because they tend to shape, direct, and limit our opportunities. Generally speaking, the lower the social classes to which we belong, the more limited our opportunities are. However, because we conventionally and habitually tend to deny the influential strength of our social standing on our opportunities and accomplishments, we need to develop social intelligence so that we can carefully assess the reality of this impact on the quality of our lives.

Social class pressures can keep us in place, especially when we allow others' perceptions and expectations to restrict our actions.

However, we can use our SI to neutralize this tendency by allowing it to prompt us to question social class standards at all times, as well as the goals we want to achieve. Our goals thus direct our actions toward maintaining the status quo, or encourage social mobility and increased social justice.

One of the most effective ways to break out of the tyranny of social class influences is to use our social intelligence to establish more meaningful conditions for all people in society. When we deliberately aim to accomplish this kind of change, and work collectively, rather than individually, toward such an end, our contributions increase opportunities for social mobility and justice. At best, this strategy improves some of the more harsh living conditions of the masses in society in the long run. Non-hierarchical relationships, far from being an unattainable ideal, appear to be a necessary precondition for creating more open, diverse, and inclusive communities in today's rapidly changing society. Social intelligence is a useful tool that makes this shift in entrenched social arrangements more likely to be achieved.

Some less developed societies may be so bound by tradition and culture that their social classes are essentially castes. Social castes predictably restrict social mobility so much that it is exceedingly difficult for any individuals or groups to modify the rigid social hierarchies in these societies. In caste societies, individual and group opportunities are passed down through the generations, without any significant modification through time. Thus castes are very rigid, closed social classes, which are an extreme form of social stratification. Caste characteristics in social conditions are not limited to less industrialized societies. Some significant rudiments of caste systems can be found in contemporary industrial social class systems, such as institutionalized racism and sexism.

Wherever class differences are highly institutionalized, as in the cases of gender, sexual orientation, and economic contrasts, there may be very little social mobility. However, in caste societies, or in societies with rigid and highly institutionalized class differences, social intelligence also gives us the capacity to think more clearly and, consequently, to act more deliberately toward opening up even rigid social hierarchies. There is always some room for change in the social complexities of society, and social intelligence is an organizing principle that can help us to begin to accomplish this.

VII. Social Class and Social Intelligence

Starting Points

Our social class origins are a significant source for understanding the social qualities of our being. Social class structures existed in the world well before we were born, and they have a powerful shaping impact on how we are introduced to ourselves, to groups, and to society. We are not born into a vacuum, and the resources and cultures of our social classes establish various limits and expectations for our lives.

All settled societies have some kind of social class system. This also means that throughout the entirety of our recorded history, social class has been a key player in the kinds of changes and transformations that societies have undergone. We are who we are in part because of the social ordering and arrangements we experience in our private and public lives.

Even though social classes are a recurring characteristic and condition of our past and present existence, this does not mean that we are fatalistically determined to continue to live in social hierarchies. When we use our social intelligence, we are at least able to think about and dream up alternatives to social class systems, and to try to put new kinds of social class structures into place.

First and foremost, social progress has occurred because societies have allowed their members to become socially mobile, that is to be sufficiently free to get out of the ruts of repeating what their parents, grandparents, and ancestors did before them. Sometimes this significant change occurs because education becomes more widespread, and sometimes because there are more random, uncontrolled historical circumstances like invasions or forced migrations. Whatever the precipitating events in this change, the capacity to leave the social circumstances of one's birth and immediate heritage is an important aspect of freedom, and social intelligence makes us more aware of how to go about making this start.

Whether or not classlessness is an ideological or ideal goal, what is significant is that individuals, groups, and societies need to work toward making classlessness a reality. Social intelligence suggests that for long term security and well-being, societies should be fluid or flexible rather than rigid, and able to adapt to rapid social change, rather than be static or stagnant. In these respects, conditions for both classlessness and social mobility are objectives which promote the good health of a society. We breed less discontent and decrease alienation when there are sufficient opportunities for all of us to at least aim meaningfully toward achieving the good life.

We may or may not be aware of what our social class membership is. Also, we may imagine or estimate where we are in society's hierarchy without simultaneously being grounded in reality. Whatever our awareness and imaginings are, however, we are always subjected to the power of others' views of our social class memberships. Because of this condition of being a member of society, we benefit from using social intelligence to make more accurate assessments of our social placements. When we realize the extent to which our perceptions about ourselves and our social standing are realistic, and how social class structures influence our thoughts, feelings, and behavior, we become freer to pursue our own goals and to be fulfilled.

Social intelligence includes an ability to assess our social status more or less objectively. We use the distilled knowledge of SI to guide our understanding about the ways in which people interact due to their social classes. When we have sufficient clarity to realize the strength of the influences that social classes have on our lives, we are less likely to become victims of their influences, and less likely to orient our behavior toward achieving social class ideals rather than our own ideals. SI increases our autonomy and free agency in society, which enables us to resist or transcend conventional pressures to conform to social class definitions of achievement.

We are born into a specific set of social circumstances, and ideally we go out into the world to move away from these initial limits on our behavior. Life is expansive, and we live more fully when we embrace ever-broadening social realities. However, in this process, it is beneficial to remember our social origins, and to assess our progress away from these starting points by frequently referring to this baseline. Social intelligence helps us to understand the social class dimensions of this important trajectory, and enables us to come full circle—back to our vital starting points—with considerably greater strength.

Social Stability

When we deliberately apply social intelligence to the specific tasks of our daily routines, and to how we continue to live within our everyday realities, we have a better understanding of what influences social classes have on us. This understanding enables us to deal more effectively with our own social classes. Because social intelligence includes an assessment of the functions of social classes in society at large, we can identify the transforming qualities that social class perspectives have on our understanding of all kinds of situations.

In addition to being channels for the expression of material and non-material conflicts, social class differences create a semblance of social order in society. This means that social classes establish a reasonably reliable framework for us as individual and social reference points, as well as some fairly predictable ways for members and groups of a specific society to interact. Thus social classes are a meaningful context of our individual lives, even though they essentially limit opportunities for many members of society.

Part of the problem of the rigidity and persistence of social classes throughout history is related to real individual and social needs for regularity in their social exchanges. People have to find ways to develop a shared capacity to be able to count on basic established social expectations, in order to proceed with their everyday personal and business matters. Society cannot run smoothly without at least some broad social structures in place, and class systems serve this purpose.

On the other hand, besides these fairly positive sounding outcomes, social classes also create the kinds of class conditions that easily increase individual and social experiences of relative deprivation, grievance, and alienation. However, in spite of these built-in disadvantages to social classes, it is sensible and advantageous to learn how to capitalize on one's individual position within a class structure. This application of social intelligence may ultimately increase an individual's social mobility, or deliberately shift that person's social class affiliation.

Social mobility is easier to achieve in developed societies than in less developed societies, because less developed societies are relatively unchanging. Pioneers in becoming socially mobile, whatever the social contexts, predictably help others to follow suit. By forging opportunities to make changes in the givens of social situations, we increase our own as well as others' freedom, and strengthen our autonomy in relation to social class dictates. Social intelligence guides us to recognize strategic possibilities for individual and social change. This means that when we are continuously aware of the impact that social classes have on our behavior, and at the same time act autonomously, ultimately we are sufficiently empowered to increase our individual and collective social mobility.

Social intelligence helps us to design strategies to make innovations in class structures. This is because SI is a source of knowledge of the dynamics of social classes that underlie the apparent stability and persistence of ongoing social arrangements. Recognizing the competitive social class basis of capitalism in modern industrial society, for example, helps us to see that society is stable only insofar as current class dynamics are upheld and maintained. Privilege in upper social classes depends on some degree of subordination of lower social classes. Furthermore, it is frequently these very inequalities among social classes that serve to fix society and keep it in a relatively predictable, even static, condition. Stability is not often accompanied by equality.

Thus, in many vital respects, what appears to be social stability may not be stable at all. One shift in the social class dynamics of a society can upset the given class system. Similarly, even one pioneering effort to achieve equality among social classes has an impact on the whole, often with the result that at least slow, gradual change toward increased social mobility comes into being.

Even though social stability is not frequently thought of as an individual goal for achievement in society, continuing to do business as usual is very likely to have the effect of maintaining the status quo. It takes deliberate efforts to accomplish innovation and change in both individual lives and in society at large. Social intelligence helps us to see these important, complex social nuances, and to take advantage of present situations in order to accomplish more desirable and more just individual and social outcomes for the future.

Labeling

If we are happy to identify ourselves as belonging to a low social class, this label may not sustain the power of others' labels, or their particular ways of identifying our social class situations. Even though it may seem that our families' and friends' perceptions of our social standing do not affect our behavior, their expectations can become self-fulfilling prophecies, which predictably elicit certain responses and behaviors from us.

VII. Social Class and Social Intelligence

Frequently the labels of different social classes that are given to us by others create pathways or patterns for us to follow. When our resistance to these labels, which prove to be controls of sorts, is weak, these labels have an impact on many facets of our behavior. Dismissing someone as "upper class" can lead to a shunning of that person by people in lower social classes, while at the same time this "upper class" person may be approached by individuals who want to become members of the upper class themselves. In any event, social class labels make a significant difference in how we see ourselves as well as in how others see us.

When we use social intelligence to help us to disentangle some of the unwelcome labels in our own lives, we realize more fully the extent to which labeling is a convenient way to simplify the complexity of our relationships. Labeling is also used to make our own positions more secure. Some of our labeling is synonymous with blaming or praising, which have strong emotional impacts especially because the interactive component in our social conditioning makes us label the people we like or dislike most. Labeling, in these different modes and more, is used largely to clarify who we think we are, and to try to control the unknowns of social situations. For example, social labels which are related to broad categories of social classes, such as gender and race, have many nuances that can be interpreted in infinite ways.

From the point of view of social intelligence, labeling is thought of as a kind of projection of our personal and social worlds on to others. We may project idealistic or romantic images in our social class labels, or we may project venom, as in hate speech and crimes. Because the sources of our projections are social as well as individual, and relate directly to our own social statuses, our labels can help us to rise out of unpleasant or limiting circumstances. When we label others as lower class, we feel superior; when we label others as upper class, we may feel more authentic in our positions of lower status. However, those whom we label negatively may receive significant harmful individual and social consequences from our labels. This is especially true if the social class labels we bestow are related to race, ethnicity, gender, sexual orientation, or religion.

Social intelligence helps us to be aware of the power others' labels have over our well-being, and enables us to realize the importance of relying on our own constructive labels of ourselves.

We are better able to drown out the impact of others' views of our social class or social category when we come to believe more firmly in the meanings of our own labels for ourselves. When we use our labels of ourselves to help us to carve out our niches in our everyday routines, we are less affected by how others position us in the social streams of our give and take activities. Also, to the extent that we can make these labels of ourselves transcend the more trivial aspects of our necessary social class memberships, the more likely we are to be able to be our real selves. If we want to accomplish certain goals or tasks, we can imagine ourselves as players in a particular sphere of activity, so that our key social class label becomes that of achiever rather than mere member of the middle class or upper class.

Social intelligence guides us in sorting out which labels are the most meaningful for us, and which labels give us the kind of social honor we prize most. Such a label can become a powerful source of motivation to behave in ways that transcend our social class limits. When we do this, we at the same time increase our immunity to others' rigid or narrow labels of us. Strengthening our abilities to choose our own labels gives us increased freedom and latitude in our personal relationships, in our communities, and in society.

Changing the Pecking Order

Social intelligence helps us to understand what appear to be the processes of social ordering in our communities and in society, and to confirm the durability and power of social class systems. Historical records show that social classes have had a direct impact on major events for long periods of time, and that specific kinds of social class systems have a history in their own right. Social classes within and among different species of animals have been researched by natural scientists, and the ranking behavior of these species has been tracked by examining distinctive patterns of animal behavior. Some researchers have concluded that ranking is a primary principle of interaction and organization, which characterizes primates and other members of the animal kingdom, and that rudimentary forms of social classes can result from animals' instinctive or innate behavioral tendencies.

However, the conclusions of historians and natural scientists which suggest the inevitability of social classes—especially when

VII. Social Class and Social Intelligence

their findings are applied to social classes among humans—are controversial and necessarily remain tentative. Among those who challenge historical and biological forms of determinism—particularly in their applications to human behavior—are historians and scientists who insist that we have some important lessons to learn about the malleability of human nature and the human condition from history as well as from social animals and insects.

Social intelligence does not reinforce the idea that ranking among human beings is innate or necessarily here to stay, but rather emphasizes the reality that social classes are powerful and important, have to be dealt with, and have to be understood as fully as possible. Biological explanations have their limitations in their applications to social class concerns, because we have several historical examples and series of recorded facts about how social class structures have changed through time, and how it is possible to move from being an elitist society to becoming more democratic. Whether these modifications are made among the upper classes of a particular society, or among that same society's lower classes, is not as crucial a factor as the fact that this kind of change in class structures is possible.

Social intelligence is a comprehensive summation of information and knowledge that also suggests that these principles of form and change in social classes apply to a wide range of different kinds of social classes. That is, social classes can be thought of and organized in terms of economics, political power, race, ethnicity, religion, gender, sexual orientation, or physical abilities. Although definitions of social classes are fluid and constantly in flux, the individual and group interactions which derive from hierarchical organizations of groups have some regular, distinctive patterns.

Therefore, if we choose to apply social intelligence in our everyday lives to improve our functioning and the quality of the contributions we make to others, what can we expect? First, we must become more aware of the social classes and other hierarchies of social groups in our everyday life. Next, we need to be able to recognize the many times in the course of a day when we are faced with some kind of social class challenge or dilemma. Our improved understanding of the complexities of different kinds of social classes, through making deliberate use of our social intelligence, enables us to be more consistent and creative in our responses to these powerful defining influences. SI helps us to be thoughtful rather than merely reactive in our responses to social classes. Also, when we try to change the many ways in which social classes impinge on our everyday lives, SI can guide our efforts, as well as help us to predict the kind of fall-out that may result from our efforts to change social classes.

When we use social intelligence to guide us through the many complex situations created by social classes in our lives, we will be able to assess more accurately how others will respond to us. Because other people's short term emotional security tends to be threatened by our moves to change the pecking order of our daily routines, those who are most directly affected by our strategies will resist our attempts to do things differently, and may band together to overwhelm or neutralize our initiatives. It is easy for us to give in to this kind of strong resistance. However, when we use social intelligence as a reliable and constant guide, we are able to persist in our efforts, so that we can make a real contribution to our goal to free up or level the social hierarchies that limit all of us.

Redefining the Situation

Using social intelligence to counteract the strong and complex influences of social classes in our daily lives is a transforming experience. When we limit, neutralize, or even essentially remove the impact of social class limitations in our present situations, we are more able to assess who we are and what it is that we really want to achieve. Making social class influences less powerful frees us to be who we really want to be, and to achieve what we really want to achieve.

Social intelligence also allows us to see social classes for what they are. For example, we may have followed a particular line of study or work in order to achieve a higher social status. Or we may have worshipped in a religion with a particular style largely to preserve our social honor. In addition, we may have unwittingly pursued what we believed—only from our own social class perspective—was morally right in order to essentially uphold a status quo of inequity and injustice. All of these limiting situations can now be redefined and changed through using social intelligence, because it offers us a fresher and broader perspective from which to observe and define our possibilities.

VII. Social Class and Social Intelligence

Given the freeing impact of neutralizing social class biases and lenses in our definitions of social reality, we are able to redefine our everyday situations and opportunities in more enlightened ways through using social intelligence. Although we must remain ever vigilant of our shared social tendencies to apply conventional social class standards to whatever we do, we can be relieved of the constancy and coercive impact of this pressure in our habitual thinking and behavior. Our beginning points can now become aspects of our autonomy and freedom, rather than the nexus of our allegiance to others' standards, ideals, and goals.

This broader and more enlightened perspective on who we are and what we want to do removes the compelling necessity to be socially mobile. We do not need to strive to rise in a social stratification system that no longer has a determining influence over our actions. Consequently, we can completely redefine what we want to achieve in our own lives according to those values that we cherish the most. In doing this, we automatically drop whatever we think are social hypocrisies, and we proceed more directly to accomplish new goals which express what we believe in most.

We must, however, continue to strive to be compassionate human beings in all of the varied accomplishments that minimize social class differences. Social intelligence is a more objective source of knowledge than ethnocentric or biased class-based knowledge. Because of this, social intelligence is better able to show us how to be truly compassionate in our interactions with others, while conducting our everyday lives more effectively. We no longer need to use the double or triple standards derived from different social classes in order to direct what we do, but rather we need to persist in being as objective as possible according to the principles of social intelligence.

The perspective that SI brings to bear on our day-by-day situations allows us to engage with the broadest social contexts of our lives, and thereby to see the links between who we are as individuals, groups, and societies. We do not exist in a vacuum, so the presence and being of others remains a primary concern in any socially intelligent assessment of how to understand, interpret, and act in a given situation. We continue to need SI to increase our meaning and purpose in making decisions to contribute to others, as well as to improve the quality of our own lives. Our social intelligence guides us in redefining each new situation in our everyday lives along the lines of social contexts, personal and professional relationships, and freedom.

Redefining our situations is tantamount to making a fresh start in our lives. We must realize, and act on, the fundamental potential of social intelligence to rearrange our values, priorities, and attitudes about the basics of our lives. When we do this, those people and things that seemed all too familiar to us when we were caught up in the grip of social class thinking may become more positive and yielding in their daily influences. We will no longer be threatened or challenged by our family, friends, and coworkers in the same ways that we used to be, and we will have considerably more energy to accomplish the important task of making contributions to others.

World Views

Social intelligence shows us that historically social class has served as a gateway to the rest of the world. In the normal course of affairs, we see our life chances and our possibilities for becoming players on the world stage through the lenses of our social classes. Unfortunately, however, this view of our social realities is often diminished or biased by the social class origins of our perceptions.

Because of the limiting impact of social class for most people, whatever their position in a given societal hierarchy, it is essential to at least recognize these restrictions and distortions, and what they do to our attitudes, goals, and accomplishments. Therefore, one of the most important things that social intelligence can help us to know is the extent to which our world views are influenced by ideas and beliefs which characterize our social classes, and the specific ways in which these influences and limitations are manifested.

When we change our loyalty to our social class orientations, we shift our allegiances and the assumptions we have routinely made about the world, the order of things in it, and people in the world. When we apply social intelligence to understanding our social classes, we gradually leave our more habitual interpretations behind, and move into relatively new territory. This means that our links to our families, religions, cultures, and politics or histories are permanently changed when we deliberately loosen the claims that our social classes had over our goals and priorities.

VII. Social Class and Social Intelligence

Knowing how to get free of our social class influences, and subsequently freeing ourselves, broadens our views and makes our worlds larger than they were before. Through using social intelligence we become more aware of how families are different from each other, how beliefs conflict and contrast, how education changes our roles in culture, and how we can become more active in political and historical change. We are able to link our individual selves to broader society in more dynamic ways because our world views have changed, and consequently we participate more fully and more meaningfully in our communities and societies. Action follows vision, and our extended, flexible world views are excellent preparations for consolidating more strategic and more effective social contributions.

Part of our fresh start in moving beyond social class ways of thinking, through using our social intelligence, is cultivating a capacity to see the world as being in need of freedom. Social classes are everywhere, throughout various places and times, and we need to make a fresh start, collectively rather than individually, if the world is to really be a better place for future generations.

To the extent that we can deliberately build a compelling vision of how the world could be without the more pernicious influences of social classes, we will also predictably be inspired to accomplish the goal of bringing such a world into being. When we are more aware of the limitations and restrictions that social classes bestow on us in order for them to exist, we are in a better position to act in ways that will reduce the power of social classes. Minimizing social class differences in everyday life can be a very meaningful primary goal; this goal can also nurture and guide us as we attempt to achieve it.

The most liberating view of the world that we could put together would take into account the necessity of reducing social class differences among groups or classes such as religions, races, ethnic groups, genders, sexual orientations, and physical abilities as well as economic classes. We label and create social classes in many complex ways, so that all these tendencies to rank or order need to be neutralized. We need to aim at creating the best of all worlds, and to make this vision a reality rather than let it remain a utopian dream. Such a difficult accomplishment requires that we use our social intelligence, which enables us to strive for these ideals, while dealing wisely with a wide variety of powerful and challenging everyday social realities.

VIII. Culture and Social Intelligence

Although society is made up of many different cultures, it is also fairly accurate to say that each society has a dominant culture within which other kinds of culture are situated. As we become more diverse and more open in our social arrangements, a wider range of alternative cultures can be found within or in addition to a society's dominant culture. We can also go so far as to say that each family and enduring group develops its own way of doing things—its own culture—through time, and that these pockets of culture may fit neatly or be a mismatch with the broader social culture.

Social intelligence allows us to see cultures and their different components more clearly, especially with respect to defining the many ways in which cultures accommodate or conflict with each other. We use SI to help us to single out the ideas, values, beliefs, stereotypes, ideals, religions, laws, educational goals, and other complex aspects of our cultures, and to guide us in making changes in our own participation in culture.

We are often so strongly influenced by the values of our cultures that we do not realize the extent to which culture defines our assumptions. Social intelligence gives us the ability to describe and explain cultures and cultural patterns, as well as lets us see and assess where we are in relation to mainstream values. These significant capacities ultimately enable us to know ourselves better, and therefore to make more crucial or innovative contributions to our communities.

In this process of putting ourselves directly into cultural contexts, we need to ponder seriously to what extent our values and beliefs serve us well; to understand which of our ideals may block us from being creative and productive; and to find practical ways to change the negative ways in which culture influences us. We benefit from knowing whether we have central, mainstream goals, for example, or whether we are inclined to push the envelope and move toward changing the status quo. Social intelligence clarifies the values we have and want to express; it also helps us to create more effective means to achieve our most cherished objectives.

There are some critical aspects of culture that seem to affect the quality of our individual and collective lives more powerfully than others. For example, the ideas we cherish might be thought of as our spirit or essence, and the ideals that express the national culture we live in can be thought of as a national identity. We are these kinds of ideas and ideals, and our behavior is motivated by both their strongest values and by other compelling cultural beliefs.

The assumptions we make about our daily lives, especially about other people and what we expect from them, are directly linked to the intrinsic hierarchy of our beliefs and values. Human beings are cultural beings, and we become human by absorbing values through our interpersonal exchanges with our cultures. What we take for granted—though this usually remains largely unquestioned—has a strong influence on how we act each day.

Thus our deeply-held beliefs tend to govern what we do. We benefit from using social intelligence to make us more aware and more deliberate about what we believe, but we cannot escape the reality and necessity of having to prioritize our beliefs, that is, to make some of our beliefs more important to us than others. In this respect we all live according to our individual credos, which are inextricably linked to the different cultures at large.

One way out of being the pawns of the beliefs we hold, but may not actually want to hold, is to make every effort to educate ourselves about the different kinds of values and priorities we can nurture. Sometimes we pick up clusters of values in religions or ideologies, but often we mix and match those values that have the deepest meanings for us.

If we want to understand which values are current, and what we are up against because of our existence in a shared cultural context, we can scrutinize sources such as the media. Although we do not get truth and reality through the diverse cultural expressions of the media, social intelligence helps us to use these sources to observe and assess more accurately how group influences distort and stereotype different aspects of our lives. This is an important awareness to have, and being socially intelligent allows us to see and act in more detached ways than would be possible if we did not question these cultural reflections in the media.

It is important for us to understand culture because cultures uphold all of our social classes and shared definitions of reality. We are cultural beings, as well as social beings, and everywhere we turn we see and experience culture. Although it is extremely difficult to change our social class structures, we can become motivated to change them through our cultures. We can also make changes in our own belief systems. Culture is thus a moving force for both creating social structures and changing them.

Do Ideals Matter?

Social intelligence shows us that our ideals derive from our cultures or from our shared values and beliefs. Our ideals influence how we behave and how our lives turn out, whether we know it or not, and whether we like this or not. Our ideals vary widely, and may be related to religion, education, politics, gender, science, health, or other areas of significant social concern. One of the most important common denominators among our many social ideals is that they are visionary, and they frequently point the way to a better future for all. Therefore, our ideals do not reflect what exists, but rather focus on, and draw attention to, what could be the best of all worlds.

Ideals can be inspirational, but at the same time they may contradict each other. What seems to be ideal for one person, or a particular group, may not be ideal for another. However, in most situations our ideals make worthwhile goals, because they show some kind of direction and purpose for everyday behavior that might otherwise be random or meaningless.

Because ideals help us to take a more accurate aim when we try to make our most important community contributions, they are vital to social action. Ideals suggest or even produce particular kinds of behavior that flow directly from them. Because of this tremendous power, ideals such as patriotism are a major concern for the governance of society. Agreement and solidarity among groups and individuals frequently depend on the kinds of ideals that are most widely shared. Therefore, in principle, ideals are of great social consequence and import, and they have the power to define significant aspects of the quality of life for many people in society.

On an individual basis, articulating our own ideals galvanizes us into action. We increase our sense of agency when we strive for our own authentic ideals, and we become even more motivated to achieve our goals when we work with others toward achieving similar ideals. Social intelligence confirms that sharing ideals creates social bonds, which frequently empower individual efforts. This means that we can achieve more by aligning our ideals with others than when we work alone.

Social intelligence shows us how our ideals influence social arrangements and the quality of social life in society. Understanding the relationship between ideals and behavior helps us to achieve what we value most. When we deliberately nurture the kind of ideals that mean the most to us, we are more able to change our behavior, so that it becomes directly aligned with the direction of our ideals. Also, when we deliberately nurture the kind of ideals that we share with others, we are more able to work together toward increasing the common good. Collective strategies based on shared ideals are more powerful, and therefore more effective, than individual efforts based on ideals.

We have more choices than we imagine in selecting our ideals, in cherishing, nurturing, and allowing our ideals to guide and direct our lives toward achieving increased meaningfulness for us and for others. Social intelligence heightens our awareness about the available choices of ideals, and shows us how we can either merely fit into cultural molds, or transcend established ways of doing things by creating innovative pathways to a better future.

We live in historical times when traditional cultural forms are being replaced by modern values. This major transition in our civilization produces ambiguities and contradictions in our culture, which make it more difficult to select ideals that are going to make a real difference in the change itself, or in expediting these change processes.

Social intelligence guides us to those social spheres that can yield the most meaningful ideals for us, given our own particular backgrounds and strengths. If we are being educated, for example, we might choose to honor the ideals of integrity and experience in the learning process. Actively coordinating our ideals allows us to build knowledge that has already been proved through practical, everyday use, rather than knowledge that is elitist. Furthermore, the current major shifts from traditional to modern cultures require us to use ideals from several intellectual disciplines, rather than from one or two establishment-oriented disciplines, if we are to adapt successfully to complex, disorienting social conditions.

Cultural Routines

Cultural routines are what we do each day which, whether we know it or not, help to keep us connected to society's mainstream values and traditions. We may be comfortable or uncomfortable while we accomplish these behaviors, and social intelligence shows us some of the ways in which we are limited or freed by what we do. Although cultural routines are, almost invariably, rigorous influences and controls on our behavior, they can be changed.

We conduct our usual business according to surprisingly widely shared guidelines and predictable social expectations. We do this because at a deep level we respond to the binding power of laws, social customs, and conventions defining how we should behave in acceptable, often effective ways. For example, we follow cultural ways of doing things when we meet new people, go on a job interview, come up with gender responses, or grieve. Social intelligence helps us to realize that almost no set of circumstances exists without some cultural blueprint that outlines what is required of us in thought, word, and deed. It is particularly in these ways that our everyday lives are deeply intertwined with cultural norms or standards; they serve both as stations of security and as coercive restraints on what we consider to be our options.

Social intelligence enables us to see some of the complexities of these compelling cultural influences on how we behave. First we need to recognize the interrelationships and overlaps in the different kinds of culture that exist. Next, we need to understand what our own positions are in mainstream and other cultures. Finally, we also need guidance from social intelligence in answering basic questions. How are our lives coerced and restricted by our cultures? What are some of the strongest benefits and most severe disadvantages that come from belonging to different cultures?

Social Intelligence in Everyday Life

When we think of our most entrenched cultural routines as being directly tied to the past, we can consider more carefully how traditional ways of doing things are perpetuated in today's world. These continuing cultural influences are more easily thought of as limiting change and our options for the future, than newer cultural ways of doing things that are best described as modern, flexible, and innovative. However, even though we have culturally prescribed ways in which to start and proceed to do things differently, our pioneering pathways need not be directly linked to previously established ways of doing things.

Social intelligence can help us to formulate new cultural routines, which should ultimately serve us better than those which were set up to meet past needs or prior social conditions. We move with the times more easily when we use SI as a guide to discern what works best for us and other people in the present and in the future. Even though our innovations may not be tied to the past in obvious ways, social intelligence is intrinsically a compendium of social knowledge that is made up of past experiences.

Cultural routines include how we deal with people who have different racial and ethnic heritages from ourselves, with those who have contrasting sexual orientations, and with immigrants from distant countries or contrasting civilizations. Globalization is taking place at an alarming pace, and because of our unavoidable interdependence with other countries and peoples, we need to formulate ways of interacting that honor cultural differences, preserve our own cultures, and at the same time allow us to work effectively toward establishing a meaningful global community. Cultural routines are useful ways to assess and navigate important social realities, which also need to be understood as fully as possible through using social intelligence.

In the same ways that we can increase our autonomy in relation to our original social classes, we can also loosen the hold that our habitual cultural routines have on the quality of our everyday lives. When we deliberately choose the values we want to express on a daily basis, we inevitably maintain higher levels of individual and social awareness. We are then in a position to be able to define truth and meaning according to principles we believe in, and we become sufficiently strong to break out of the ways in which we have behaved most consistently over the years if we wish to do so. We do this by selecting and cultivating group affiliations that increase our autonomy, such as particular professional associations. In this respect, we are more likely to pursue goals that inspire the deepest meanings and directions for new cultural routines.

Creeds and Priorities

Culture is the supreme source of our most deep-seated beliefs and meaningful priorities. We rank our personal and professional preferences according to these beliefs and priorities, and we act accordingly.

Throughout history and our lifetimes, we develop what can be thought of as secular creeds about the way things are, the way we are, and what should be done in the world. These kinds of belief systems inevitably generate social priorities, with the result that there is a direct link between what we understand to be important and what we deliberately aim to do with our lives. Thus our priorities are a strong influence on our behavior, and the more consistent our beliefs are, the more effective we shall be in accomplishing our priorities.

Social intelligence helps us to know what our deepest beliefs are, and therefore what our priorities should be in our behavior in order to be true to those beliefs. When we recognize the extent to which we have acted according to the influence of particular cultural values, we are more able to sort out what our goals should be. We get to know ourselves more fully when we examine what we have done in the past, and what kind of value choices have shaped our actions into the present day.

If we want to change our priorities, which can revolutionize the way we conduct ourselves and deal with others, we need to make deliberate shifts in our most significant principles or deepest beliefs. It is only when we revise what we think is most important that we can reestablish our priorities and transform our goals.

At every point along the way of making this kind of fundamental change in how we conduct our lives, our cultures continue to influence what we think is important, what we believe about our current situations, and what we want to accomplish. In order to think creatively outside of cultural limitations, we need to be more objective and more expansive in our vision of possibilities, and to make different cultural choices. Social intelligence connects us to cultural sources for accomplishing these goals.

Social Intelligence in Everyday Life

Our priorities influence our life outcomes because, for better or for worse, they shape and largely determine our behavior. The choices we make every day depend on what our priorities are, and the patterns of our priorities structure our daily behavior. All of these influences operate within and derive from our cultures. There is no way for us to completely liberate ourselves from the pervasiveness of our cultural influences.

When we leave home to travel into unfamiliar territory and foreign cultures, we suffer a certain amount of culture shock. Essentially this is the experience of having our assumptions snatched from us, with an automatic substitution of contrasting values and priorities. Sometimes this kind of fundamental disorientation is so powerful that it makes us unable to fill our usual social roles, with the immediate result that we become more or less dysfunctional in the new cultural setting. For example, when we do not know the language of a foreign country, we are unable to conduct ourselves as usual. When this kind of culture shock is associated with immigrant hardships and related experiences, the dramatic cultural challenges may handicap us for a lifetime.

Social intelligence shows us the significance of recognizing, understanding, and using cultural cues in our communications with others. We need to become sufficiently familiar with our cultures in order to function well, and certainly in order to achieve our goals. Culture is the water we swim in, and we have to know different ranges of beliefs and priorities so that we can make sense of our social conditions and be truly selective and effective in what we do.

Now that the world is becoming a smaller place through increased travel and improved communications, we are experiencing what seems to be a convergence among some cultures, and at the same time a more extreme and exaggerated differentiation among other cultures. We recognize a global economy, but it is still difficult for us to think in terms of a global culture and a global community.

Even though a few values are shared by most cultures, including sharply contrasting cultures, each civilization necessarily has its own distinctive values, opportunities, and priorities. Therefore, unless we deliberately build cultural creeds, for example, about international human rights or a global ethic, we will not be able to bind global citizens together in important and meaningful ways. If we cannot achieve this kind of cultural change, we will have to continue to try to coexist with contradictory, conflicting, and sometimes completely incompatible local and global priorities.

VIII. Culture and Social Intelligence

Educating Ourselves

Education puts us in direct contact with the past, present, and future. We are invited to see the world through cultural products representing many different perspectives, disciplines, skills, and ways of knowing. We learn how to be civilized rather than barbaric, and how to work toward increasing the common good for all. In recent times education has become the cultural product par excellence that increases democracy, civic participation, and freedom.

In our present day society, an ideal of lifelong learning is touted as one of the most meaningful goals to strive for by many different kinds of educational institutions. This emphasis signals a new public awareness that formal learning for a few limited years is both inadequate and insufficient. However advanced the achievement levels attained through academic degree programs, they are regarded merely by some people as specific credentials rather than as a true education.

In this relatively new venture of lifelong learning, it has become increasingly apparent that we need to learn how to learn as well as what to learn. Only by understanding how we learn and what we need to know can we deepen and broaden our understanding of the world on a continuing basis. These skills are vital if we are to survive and do well in today's society.

Being able to educate ourselves about our culture is a crucial component of any satisfactory plan for lifelong learning. We must learn from others, but we also need to be constantly in charge of as many of our educational options and decisions as possible. When we can steer ourselves into those learning situations that we believe are most beneficial to us, we are better able to enrich our lives as well as the social conditions of others.

Social intelligence offers some pointers on what it means to educate ourselves. Education of any kind is a social and cultural product, which meets some individual needs and has distinct social uses and purposes. Educational resources and sources of knowledge are integral parts of the cultural base of society, and they reflect diverse social interests and hierarchical statuses within culture. We draw distinctions between high culture and popular culture, for example, which represent alternative sources of knowledge and different perspectives for educating ourselves. When we opt to learn high culture, we gradually make inroads into traditional mainstream society. By contrast, when we opt to learn popular culture, we tend to gravitate to more peripheral or less powerful social positions.

Social intelligence itself can be thought of as an important result of educating ourselves. When we stay alert to recognizing and understanding the complexity of social influences in our everyday lives, we essentially learn the extent to which history, social conditions, and established social institutions benefit or harm our well-being. Gaining the distinctive practical knowledge of social intelligence is thus an essential way to educate ourselves, so that we become more adept at recognizing at least some of the vital links between our individual human agency and the processes of broad social change.

When we do not choose to educate ourselves, or when we do not see how we can continue to educate ourselves, our knowledge becomes stagnant and unrelated to our day-to-day social situations. We compartmentalize our lives and activities without realizing that this separation of knowledge and practice makes our education relatively worthless for meeting real needs, whether they be our own or those of other people. Therefore, in order to truly educate ourselves, we must first be committed to the possibility of combining learning with practice, so that we can more effectively absorb new ideas with their individual and social implications.

Educating ourselves within our cultures is one of the most direct and valuable avenues for bringing about change. Education makes us aware of our ideals, goals, and aspirations, and at the same time gives us a clearer sense of history. By contrast, ignorance is one of the strongest enemies of freedom. Social intelligence shows us how we can deliberately educate ourselves to diminish or negate the power and social consequences of ignorance. As we learn more about who we are and who others are, we can act with increased compassion and empathy. We become whole through educating ourselves, and our enhanced social intelligence helps us to make wise moves on a daily basis.

Media Reflect Culture

If you are still asking yourself what culture is, and how you can understand different aspects of culture and cultural change, looking more closely at what we consume in newspapers, magazines, and television—to name just a few of our contemporary media—can be helpful. As never before the media allow us to observe others' feelings, thoughts, and representations of society, and also show us what local communities, societies, and international groups are thinking and doing.

Social intelligence enables us to see these immediate cultural writings and images more objectively, and to interpret their diverse symbols as indicators of the state of our current cultures. At the same time, social intelligence leads us to question and assess to what extent media reflections of culture are reality, distortions of facts, or indicators of social change.

The media present written and audio-visual materials that help us to understand cultures of the past, present, and future, together with many of their complex interdependencies and interrelationships. We have much raw cultural material before us because of the media, but we need social intelligence to guide us to be more discriminating about what meanings and values from the media we will accept into our daily realities.

Historically every culture creates its own myths and stories. They often become the subject of different kinds of contemporary media representations, including those items that are produced primarily for children. In fact, a reliable measure of values that a culture considers important is the content of the books or programs the media present to children. The signs and symbols of mainstream culture are more clearly distilled and ordered in children's media productions than in most adult media representations.

Even though today there is more public interest in facts and truth than ever before, due to increasingly widespread literacy and higher levels of education, there is still a strong shared need to retell familiar stories, or to rewrite historical themes for contemporary readers. We are consumers of culture, and in due course, culture itself is at least partially driven by the motors of individual and collective interests represented in the media. Directors, editors, and producers have sufficiently powerful positions to be able to articulate ways that may change our culture or maintain the cultural status quo. The determining factor governing these outcomes is that values in the media depend on the power of special interests.

Because media reflect and respond directly to culture, we can both observe the depth and breadth of the influence of culture through media representations, and be more critical of the ways in which we are exposed to these cultural influences. Without examining the content of some contemporary movies, for example, we might be unaware of the strength of the influence that movies have on our cultural sensitivities and vulnerabilities about gender or racial stereotypes. Furthermore, unless we develop and implement some deliberate change strategies to modify what we see and hear through the media, the media will continue to exaggerate and distort the inescapable cultural influences that shape our everyday lives.

One of the disadvantages of the close connection between culture and the media is that we can easily end up living in a dream world. We can believe that a cultural myth is factual rather than a social artifact. We can accept cultural stereotypes as acceptable definitions of our own roles and realities. Because we are enchanted and manipulated by highly developed technologies, we come to believe that artifice and conventional symbols are worthy ideals and goals.

Therefore, we are in constant danger of being lulled into complacency, or even oblivion, by some of the media expressions of our culture. It is because of the strength of this possible betrayal by our culture that we need social intelligence to see culture for what it is, and to identify the many kinds of constructive and advantageous changes that can be made to modify our more misleading cultural beliefs.

Given this dangerous scenario, social intelligence is essentially a wake-up call for us to use our socially informed critical thinking capabilities to distinguish between social fact and social fiction, to see our social conditions for what they are, and to seize our freedom in spite of the influences of stereotypes. SI helps us to break out of culturally regimented and controlled behavior, and to go forth with our lives so that we can seek the common good rather than lesser ideals. It cuts through many of the ways in which culture is used to manipulate us, as well as the ways in which people are imprisoned or at least impeded by their conventionally acceptable cultural beliefs.

Culture as Causation

Although social intelligence shows us that many social influences have a strong impact on our everyday lives, some of these influences are more important than others: social institutions; social classes; and culture. Culture in and of itself is not the primary causation of who we are and what we do, but the pervasiveness of culture is extremely powerful. Values and ideals are integral parts of social institutions and classes, as well as of cultures, and these everyday cultural influences produce our daily routines.

Culture can also be thought of as being intimately related to different aspects of society without causing them. For example, social groups and classes change through time, and frequently these important structural changes take place at the same time as shifts in the cultural mosaic of society. In short, none of these bare-bones dimensions of social processes can be understood without identifying the associations, influences, and interdependencies between social structures and culture. Culture is in the air we breathe, in our blood, and in our dreams, but it does not wholly determine our social conditions or our behavior.

In many respects, social intelligence includes awareness that it is largely the cultural underpinnings of social institutions and classes that keep these structures in place, and perpetuate their influence in our everyday lives. We frequently accomplish remarkably little change in society, due to the emotional investment that people make in their traditional ideals, expectations, and values. Social institutions such as the family, religion, the economy, education, and the political system resist innovation because order and security are felt to be of paramount importance in a rapidly changing world. Therefore we frequently choose to perpetuate the status quo partly in fear that designing our own changes will prove to be more difficult than dealing with what is. As human beings, we need a stable center to our lives, and what we are familiar with is meaningful and serves this purpose.

Social intelligence looks beyond such immediate fears or short-term reactions to possibilities for change. We discover that we can be more in charge of our individual and collective lives when we make deliberate choices to do things differently. By changing our value choices, we can innovate more successfully and effectively in our families, religions, the economy, education, and political systems, and we see that we need not be beholden to how things have been done in the past. Also, because we are advantaged in that we are less ignorant than any generation before us, we can dare to suggest innovative, if not idealistic, strategies to guide us to expand the common good.

Social Intelligence in Everyday Life

Social intelligence, although mapping out the greater effectiveness of collective efforts to make changes, also draws attention to the fact that each individual can make a real difference. We learn to recognize how culture and value choices have controlled our behavior, and to garner sufficient courage from our knowledge so that we can make a quantum leap forward wherever possible. Thus we reach new frontiers through making different kinds of value and culture choices. Choosing to become more informed, to be educated, or to pursue a career moves us in directions of being more able to increase the common good for all. As movers of change, we honor the strength of culture as a social influence without becoming victims of its allures and destructive powers.

In many ways, our understanding of culture and social intelligence brings us full circle. We know that in order to be human we must absorb many significant aspects of our culture, and yet this is not the full story. We have to become human but we also have to exercise our agency in the world, so that we can build on the social and cultural givens of our beginnings. It is only when we are strong in our individual and social selves that we can go forward and make worthwhile contributions to others. Although culture is not the sole determinant of these processes, we cannot develop our potentials and create our designs for the world without the resource and support of culture. Culture is the invaluable content of our being and fulfillment in the beginning and as an end.

IX. Society and Social Intelligence

Society affects us deeply through politics, history, evolution, and mass changes such as the human rights movement, the information revolution, or shifting gender roles. There is no way we can escape these influences, and we are changed by their impact whether we know it or not, and whether we like it or not. Social intelligence includes recognizing the importance of these influences, as well as specific power relations throughout society such as the dominance of race, class, gender, and ethnicity in ongoing social relations, exploitation, and oppression.

Deepening our understanding through social intelligence is empowering. When we can see our social limitations we, in fact, increase our autonomy, and become more able to change our relationships and social pressures in broader society. SI can also help us to create more enlightened political policies, new communities, and improved working conditions. This means that in the long run it can guide us toward creating a shared future that will be more positive for a greater number of people than that which would result from acting on blind faith in tradition or in the establishment.

The ultimate, most comprehensive source of social intelligence is society itself, whether we think of society as referring to a particular nation state or to the global community. In order to be fully human, and in order to function independently, we need to see ourselves in ever-increasing social contexts. This perspective puts us directly in touch with currents of history and our geographical roots. It is only by considering ourselves within the broadest context of society that we will be able to understand which political forces move us along in spite of our wishes, and which help to make us fully awake and active members of the world society.

Social intelligence helps us to sum up and formulate a sound perspective on global social forces. These influences tend to either hold us in place or to provide us with meaningful opportunities to be agents of social change. This broad view is not a mere product of our imaginations, but rather a way to be more objective about our own social conditions, and a means through which we can act more freely. We are who we are not only because of the immediate social influences in our surroundings, but also because of some of the most geographically remote social powers.

Society is composed of basic social structures, such as social institutions and social classes, as well as cultural traditions and practices which embody values, ideals, and priorities. We are enmeshed in these vital social currents that make it possible for a society to survive. One outcome is that we may be sufficiently limited by social structures and practices that we become victims of these same forces, or, alternatively, we may manage to retain our autonomy and be reasonably free actors in spite of the social structures and practices. Furthermore, even though we may choose to be members of small groups rather than large groups, these broader social and global influences will necessarily continue to infiltrate our being and actions.

Some social groupings carry us beyond the boundaries of nation states: blocs of countries with similar religions or cultures; international bonds of ethnicity and race; shared gender interests; and overlapping historical legacies. In each instance these units of civilization are a strong rallying point that transcends, and at the same time goes deeper than mere national interest. Also, such groupings intrinsically have broader bases of membership and participation than do nation states.

One consequence of these worldwide social trends is that society as a social unit has come to mean less in contemporary times than it did previously. Although changing national boundaries has characterized much of history, and continues today, global stretches of social arrangements have increased in importance. The fact that realistically we are now members of a global community means that there are fewer places for us to hide, and more responsibilities to be faced. We are interdependent, not only in our smallest family units, but also in our international relations. Social intelligence is much needed as a guide to help us to unsnarl these complexities, and to help us to make the world a better place.

The World and I

Thinking about ourselves in the context of the world gives us one of the broadest perspectives possible on our own individual and social situations. Deliberately creating this view is easier today than in earlier eras, largely because of the availability and easy accessibility of information about what is happening both at home and in far-off places. Social intelligence shows us that it is beneficial to have this scope of information at our fingertips, and that what is happening at the other end of the world is frequently not insignificant for us, our communities, or our societies. Keeping up with current affairs through the many media sources enables us to develop a more solid historical perspective on our lives and social conditions, so that we can take better informed action on a daily basis.

When we ponder the complexity of the links and possibilities between the world and I, we can similarly think of ourselves as being creatures of God, a speck in the eternal universe, or a mammal on Planet Earth. These particular broad contexts are less political, and more or less moral in referring to the historically and geographically bound parameters of the world. There is a relentless tangibility and earthiness to our being grounded somewhere in the world at a particular point in time, so that place and time become critical dimensions of a reality which seems to apply more directly to us than situating ourselves in the universe in general, in a relationship to a supernatural being, or in the animal kingdom.

Associating a world context with our innermost sense of self is not an illusion, but rather a fact that is frequently unrealized. For example, it is all too easy to live our entire lives without feeling or understanding any sense of kinship with people and conditions that are distant or removed from our locales. Furthermore, a lack of awareness of there being any significant link between the world and I does not appear to limit or harm individuals and groups. It is easier to make the point that when the interdependence of the world and I can be understood, it becomes possible to live at a deeper level of appreciation and with a higher level of functioning.

We make more effective contributions to less fortunate people throughout the world, for example, when we act in concert with an adequate base of knowledge about the rest of the world.

Social intelligence helps us to imagine and respond to the many complex linkages and interdependencies between our individual agencies of I and social conditions in local, national, and international communities. When we use SI as a resource, we are better able to know how to think, what to do, and how to approach others. Social intelligence helps us to redefine our responsibilities for undertaking social change, because it helps us to understand both the limits and the many possibilities of our social settings. The social conditions we need to consider include the broadest social contexts as well as the more obvious familial, domestic, or local groups. Sometimes it is these broadest social contexts that make the real difference in how we lead our everyday lives.

When we have a sufficiently deep understanding of the influences of society in setting the scene for our actions, we are more able to seize opportunities to act rather than to succumb to passivity, or to being victims of circumstances. Active or passive postures to the social conditions that face us predispose us to accomplish more or less effective goals. The more we use social intelligence to guide our understanding and actions, the more we are able to exercise independence and initiative in routine matters, or even in the most extreme hardships or crises.

The world is our oyster when we can attain this kind of freedom. Although we may become freer to travel with a broader awareness of the world and I, we do not need to travel to accomplish tasks that have direct relevance to expanding the common good of the international community. We merely need to keep our awareness sufficiently broad and current, which enables us to consider the consequences of our actions more responsibly, so that we can truly reach out to the world at large.

Moral Order in the Universe?

Social intelligence suggests that at present there is no single moral order in the universe. Religions, philosophies, ideologies, values, and norms vary dramatically in different cultural and geographical settings. We might yearn to have our own particular values universalized, but unfortunately this wish is perhaps saying little more than that we would like to control how others think and behave.

IX. Society and Social Intelligence

If we are interested in building communities that stretch outside our familiar local enclaves, we must share at least some important meanings and standards of behavior with others, which will include more than those already established and accepted in our friendly neighborhoods. Adapting successfully to our rapidly expanding world includes understanding and respecting what others believe and cherish, so that we can enter into a peaceful coexistence with them, and share responsibly in vital tasks which will increase the common good.

Some religious leaders have proposed that we should use the common denominators among the values of major world religions as the beginnings for constructing a global ethic. Moving in this direction, as well as striving for such an accomplishment, suggests that universal moral standards can be gleaned from our human and religious experiences, and that using a global ethic to guide behavior could ultimately establish at least a minimum standard for moral order in the world. However, if we use social intelligence to look at history, and to acknowledge the degree of divisiveness and conflict around religion, the best of all possible worlds may not result from trying to achieve such a goal.

The contemporary ideal of pluralism may serve us better in working toward a peaceful and respectful coexistence in the international community. In the context of pluralism there would be an acceptance of different moral orders, with sufficient understanding that common denominators of values and interests could also guide us to expand our common good through our social practices. A pluralistic design for society would avoid any coercion of non-believers into compliance with traditional religious values, and would suggest that establishing a universal moral order begins with tolerance and respect for others.

Archeological and historical evidence shows that as far as we can tell human beings have always had severe conflicts with each other; social intelligence indicates that we might fare better from being prepared to deal with this inclination as effectively as possible, rather than from trying to create what may essentially turn out to be a dream world of peace. The questions that need to be asked are: how can we deal with our given differences without imposing on others, and how can we work together productively for a common good, rather than waste our resources in unproductive and lethal conflicts.

There are other ideals, besides moral order, which also need to be considered when we think of stability in the world at large. For example, can an ideal of social justice galvanize sufficient individuals, groups, and societies to act collectively in order to make the world a better place? Can education be sufficiently independent of specific political or religious interests, in order to reduce ignorance and use knowledge to reduce human suffering and to support worthwhile endeavors?

In many respects, social intelligence suggests that human beings are all moral beings, and even that being social in our orientation to life implies having a moral awareness and concern for others, especially for those who are less privileged than ourselves. In the long run, in the interests of our own survival if not for our fulfillment, we need to work toward increasing opportunities for all. If we fail to do this, the alternative will be increased alienation, conflict, and war.

In some very real ways there is a unity among human beings. Although this is different from a moral unity, there are physiological common denominators of the human experience, and patterns of societies' development are sometimes sufficiently similar that we can make meaningful comparisons. Social intelligence attempts to understand and to take into account both similarities and uniqueness.

Whatever social conditions exist in different societies, some basic human needs seem to be similar. We are in the same boat in terms of our needs to adapt, within and among our societies, to global trends and tendencies, for example. Although moral order in the universe may be too far removed from most of our everyday realities to make this a viable goal, we need to put ourselves in the world with empathy, compassion, and concern for others, or our quality of life will be severely damaged and ultimately hazardous to our survival.

A Global Economy

At the same time that many units of society seem to get larger—at least with respect to thinking about societal connections to an international or a global community—relationships between nation states should ideally become stronger and more significant. We are connected to other societies through many different kinds of complex transactions and exchanges, and one of the accepted ways in which these connections are established is the tendency of business expansion to include trade with a growing number of foreign countries.

IX. Society and Social Intelligence

Therefore, with these conditions in mind, social intelligence shows us that at least one kind of global unity, which may not always be benign, already exists. We are all participants in a one-world economy, whether we know it or not, and whether we like it or not. Our everyday lives are inextricably tied up with strong market forces, and even though we may not have wealth or resources ourselves, we are deeply affected by market forces. For instance, pockets of poverty are frequently unintended consequences of economic prosperity and successful trade.

Many social changes are brought about by the everyday business activities of dominant economic interests in particular societies. Profit motives drive economic powers to sustain their productivity, and the consumption of goods takes on a high priority in many diverse cultural exchanges. We begin to believe that we need material possessions, and this creates very tangible kinds of expectations and practices.

Social intelligence helps us to assess the strength of economic influences on the quality of our lives; at the same time it enables us to define which human factors are not served by the unprecedented worldwide expansions of business activities. Somewhere, some people's interests are not met, and there tends to be both exploitation and oppression in order to keep up the momentum necessary for ever-increasing profits and privilege.

In the midst of the success story of capitalism there is a series of complex losses and unintended consequences. We must ask ourselves to what extent we benefit from the global economy, and to what extent we are victims of these powerful dynamics. We should also question why progress is frequently thought of in terms of consuming more goods, rather than as building a common good which would be capable of meeting at least some of the fundamental needs of all.

When market forces are out of control, which they often are, it is difficult to make effective human interventions. We are afraid to protect the less fortunate through certain kinds of legislation, for example, because we think that limiting free market forces will reduce the productivity and profits of big business, as well as reduce the willingness of people to invest their resources in new and old business ventures.

Both national and international trading patterns tend to polarize social concerns about economic freedom and human rights. Should we not build legal protections into business transactions, so that people's welfare is a higher priority than increasing profits? The harsh realities of our global economy call attention to many human issues that are at the same time both old and new.

Benefits received from our global economy are a high standard of living in some societies, with increased material assets and material goods for some people within these societies. However, we are interdependent in our relationships within and among societies, and where economic differences among groups and societies are extreme, a sense of relative deprivation inevitably increases. These conditions increase alienation, which predisposes groups and societies to conflicts and warfare.

Social intelligence suggests that importance be placed on societies to provide a sufficiently large number of opportunities for members of their populations to be upwardly mobile. When this happens, individuals cannot be unnecessarily trapped in positions that limit them and their life chances. When all or most members of a population have access to adequate levels of education, for example, there will be less alienation and less inclination toward conflict and antagonisms. Education makes social mobility possible, and, by definition, social mobility minimizes or removes social stagnation.

In the long run our global economy is a way to adapt to our environment. The environment knows no real national or societal boundaries because Planet Earth exists in its own right, and similar natural characteristics stretch across political and economic boundaries in their own inimitable ways. Although natural resources may be subjected to economic or political needs and uses, they are integral parts of the environment, having their own intrinsic reality. How we treat our environment is an economic or political issue, but the environment must be cared for if it is to survive, and if we are to survive. Looking after our environment is ultimately synonymous with making our global economy possible, especially at current rates of economic productivity in the international community.

Political Pressures

Political pressures result from the distribution of power within a society and among societies, as well as from our shared beliefs in the legitimacy of that power. Interestingly, we may not be deeply affected by political forces and influences when we do not acknowledge that they exist in the first place. We are more likely to be coerced by political pressures when we see ourselves as relatively powerless, or as needing to accommodate to society.

Social intelligence shows us that political resources may overlap with and be closely related to economic resources, and that both the political system and the economy have similar patterns, processes, and practices. However, the political system is unique and different from the economy and market forces because the political system has well-established claims to legitimacy and, consequently, because of its access to forces and controls of the state, such as the military. Political pressures are felt because of the real power of these coercive forces.

Sometimes those who hold political power in a society are members of economic and political elites. This hierarchy of power holders exerts political pressures over other members of society, deliberately keeping people in their respective social classes and restricting their social mobility.

When these kinds of political conditions reach extreme proportions, with opportunities being severely limited for most of the population, emigration rates increase as people try to leave the country. Political pressures dictate the directions of these emigrations, and those individuals who flee the political limitations and restrictions of their own societies will seek autonomy in other locales.

Population density and fertility rates may be influenced directly by policies and other kinds of political pressures. Legal systems enforce high taxes to sanction behavior which threatens the status quo, or which does not meet current state objectives. All in all, political pressures can be wielded manipulatively to benefit elites and to exploit or oppress the less fortunate in society. This situation limits or annihilates the ideal of establishing a common good for all.

Political leadership may consolidate political pressures and work toward ameliorating social conditions, but this effort may not be sustained when other individuals come into power. Social intelligence suggests that the most effective leadership possible for a society results from the development of grass roots initiatives. These are the only kinds of leadership that are strong enough to survive and transcend individual idiosyncrasies, due to the collective nature of their sources and momentum.

Social Intelligence in Everyday Life

A careful consideration of societies in a global perspective shows us that a wide variety of political regimes exists. We learn that democracy is a Western ideal, and that varied forms of rule and legitimate social arrangements are used by other societies to manage their power and their states' responsibilities. Given this wide range of political possibilities, the most critical and universal question is how individuals relate to the political powers that exist in their societies, and to what extent these political pressures limit individuals' freedoms and choices. It is in this spirit that all of us need to understand how our everyday lives are influenced and restricted by political pressures, and what we can do to change this.

Fixed and static power arrangements in societies are more difficult to live with or change than those which are flexible and have some degree of give-and-take. Competition and conflict need to be regulated in some way in all societies, whatever the political regimes, in order to accomplish the minimum of security necessary for establishing law and order in a society. We cannot afford to be pulled in a direction of war rather than peace, as this threatens the very existence of society itself, and especially the global community.

When we use social intelligence to understand what human civilization means, and at the same time focus on the nature of political arrangements in the society in which we live, we will be more empowered as individuals and communities. We need to link this awareness of the existence and power of political pressures to our everyday negotiations with others, so that we can be freer to accomplish more widespread, needed goals.

Interdependence and Change

Social intelligence includes awareness of the linkage between interdependence in society and social change. Because of the holistic system of societies and the global community, any change in one part of the whole affects all the other parts. The fact of our interdependence means that we can never act in a vacuum, and that each individual counts.

The whole of each society, and the whole of the international community, have a power that is greater than the sum of their parts. Part of being human means that we necessarily depend on the power of these broad social systems for our survival and

124

fulfillment. Furthermore, each part of each whole is so interdependent that no single part of a system can move without having a distinct impact on the whole.

Social change occurs as a consequence of the shifting of the parts in a society and in the global community. Sometimes these shifts are dramatic and rapid, bringing in their wake predictable dislocations and adaptations. Sometimes, however, these shifts and their consequences may be hidden or latent, not surfacing immediately. Even when deliberate attempts are made to change part of a society, or part of the international community, the shifts that actually occur through time may be largely unintended and unwanted.

These characteristics of different kinds of shifts, and their results, do not negate the interdependence that exists within societies and among societies in the global community. Rather, the range of social reactions, because of their unavoidability, shows that interdependence itself is alive and well, and is deeply and inextricably related to the capacity of a society or a global system to change.

The human dimension of these significant characteristics of the interdependence of society and its relationship to change is that we all need each other in our national and international relations. This need for each other is deeper than economic, environmental, and emotional dependence. Our survival, as well as the perpetuation of Planet Earth, can only be realized through safeguarding the delicate balance of our interdependence. We are in the same boat, and if we are to make it to our destinations, we must respect this vital and precious condition of the interdependence of our existence.

One way we can try to safeguard our security is to design strategies to meet social needs, so that no particular group is excluded from the common good. However, even if we plan to expand our shared resources, and to distribute them more evenly, such radical change will be difficult to implement and may backfire. First, we must use social intelligence to persuade ourselves and others that our mission to recognize our interdependence is both serious and worthwhile.

When we adapt to the automatic changes that take place in societies regardless of what our deliberate policies and strategies are, we accomplish some measure of success. We have to be sufficiently flexible to accommodate shifts in society and in the global community if we are to reach a point of thoughtfulness and awareness about which strategies will work best to bring social developments more under our control. Understanding evolution, history, and globalization through the lens of social intelligence helps us in this endeavor. When we are aware of the complexity of the different aspects of slow and speedy social changes, we will be able to assess our situations more accurately and act more effectively.

At no time should we question or doubt that individuals can have an impact on global conditions. Because we are necessarily bound to our societies and to the global community, what we decide to do and what we do can make a considerable difference to the status quo. Although societies may seem to be increasingly absorbed into the world community, with the world at the same time essentially becoming a smaller place, we are not predetermined. We can ask difficult questions about what we practice on a daily basis, and we can head off in directions of bringing about constructive changes even in what may be experienced as disastrous circumstances. This kind of initiative is our individual and social responsibility, given the seriousness and complexity of present day tensions in the world at large.

In order to think more clearly about interdependence and change, it is necessary to put our lives in the broader perspectives of our societies and the world community. These contexts of our individual existences give us more objectivity about who we are and what we can do to respond to the social limitations we see. This is a firm starting point for working toward the social ideal of preserving the best aspects of the civilizations we know. We need a sufficiently broad vision of the whole in order for us to proceed with social intelligence and wisdom. Although peaceful coexistence among societies may not be our preferred outcome, working toward this goal this will protect our needs to survive amidst the volatile interdependences and changes in our many social systems. Furthermore, peaceful coexistence can be a precondition of truly honoring the diversity of our communities, societies, and international relations.

Survival on Planet Earth

Social intelligence is an important tool for making survival on Planet Earth possible. We can only make thoughtful decisions and act responsibly in the present and future when we have an adequate understanding of the broadest aspects of society and their dynamics: politics, history, evolution, and mass changes such as the human rights movement, the information revolution, and shifting gender roles.

Social intelligence includes recognizing power relations, such as the dominance of race, class, and gender in ongoing social exchanges, exploitation, and oppression. When we are able to recognize our limitations and restrictions, we also increase our power. When we feel that we can have some kind of impact on how we live and the quality of our shared social conditions, we will be more able to change our relationships and the powerful pressures of society. Ideally, social intelligence will lead us in the direction of creating more enlightened political policies, new communities, and improved working conditions, not only in our own societies but in other societies as well. Thus we will be able to respond to both national and global needs, which will ensure a higher level of survival for all people and for our planet.

One of the ways in which social intelligence can guide us to take more enlightened action is to put our energies into designing our future, rather than merely trying to perpetuate tradition or the establishment. Although both tradition and the establishment have survived in some societies for hundreds, if not thousands, of years, and this staying power brings with it some virtue, it is also a reality that in these societies only a few, rather than the masses, are privileged through their access to resources. For the pragmatic purpose of our own survival it is important to find ways to increase the common good, so that inequalities and perceived relative deprivation will not engender alienation and conflict.

Whenever we apply social intelligence to our current situations, our survival on Planet Earth has to be our first priority. Without survival, nothing is possible. Survival promises a longer life to individuals and societies, and conditions that meet basic human needs. Survival may not bring fulfillment with it for some members or a population, but survival is a necessary precondition for anyone's fulfillment.

Environmental concerns come into view when we consider the survival of Planet Earth. Biological and physiological considerations remind us that there is a constant interplay between individuals and their environmental conditions; unless we preserve the environment, we will ultimately deplete our economic resources. In this respect, social intelligence serves as a constant reminder that we survive only when we know how to deal successfully with the laws of the universe. This is to say that social conditions also have their predictabilities: patterns of human behavior; the push and pull of power relations; and probable outcomes given predisposing tendencies and environmental conditions.

Through history and ongoing current events individuals and societies make specific contributions to others. We have to learn how to deal with clashes between civilizations as well as more domestic disputes, with a realization that what we think is personal is also political—all of our actions affect society and the world in some way.

Working toward improving the quality of life for all is a lifetime goal, which needs to be undertaken with social intelligence if our efforts are to be effective. We need to do a better job of building communities at home if there is to be a real global community. Furthermore, diversity will come to us, even if we do not deliberately seek it out, and there are always opportunities to bring new kinds of social practices into being.

We have a responsibility to orient the next generation toward accomplishing these tasks because our own lifetimes are too short to complete what has to be done. As well as being examples to those who are younger than we are, we need to perpetually strengthen our awareness of the social conditions of our existence. Planet Earth is more likely to survive when we consider carefully what needs to be done at each stage of the realization of our ideals. It is only when our shared survival needs are met that we will be able to enjoy the true richness of the world, and respect and appreciate the dazzling diversity we behold.

Future Directions

X. Making Social Intelligence Our Own

S ocial intelligence is learned. However, social intelligence is much more than an idea or a particular technique through which we are able to analyze more meaningfully the human experience. Social intelligence is a practice and a way of life that evolves primarily from our daily exchanges with others. It is a personal and deliberate kind of re-socialization that gives us a particular posture to life. Although we may see and begin to understand intellectually how social systems affect us, it is not until we have acted on the basis of this knowledge that social intelligence becomes truly our own.

Social intelligence prepares and protects us for whatever the future brings; it also helps us to deal with difficult situations, past and present. Furthermore, we can be more assured of reaching our goals, and of creating the good society, when we use and allow ourselves to be guided by social intelligence. Social intelligence helps us to construct stronger new communities in the present and future, which are based more closely on an ideal of the well-being of all. We are interdependent beings who cannot afford to take the risk of merely perpetuating already established but frequently destructive social patterns and relationships, because these will ultimately bring about our individual and collective demise.

Once we know how to cultivate social intelligence at a deep level, we are able to pass on the awareness and wisdom of social intelligence to future generations. When we make social intelligence our own, we are able to change at least some of the problematic social conditions that restrict our everyday lives in contemporary society. Because of the potential durability of the changes we can make through using the principles of social intelligence, we advance more freely and confidently into an improved future to be shared by the many, rather than a few.

Social intelligence must become an integral part of our being before we own it fully. We have to see, hear, and speak social intelligence if it is to be a strong influence on our behavior. It is only when both the rational and the emotional roots of SI take a deep hold within us that we can depend on it more fully to create benefits and changes for us and our communities.

It may take a long time before we become adequately socially intelligent, especially if we have led protected lives, or if we have been members of communities that are secluded from the hurly-burly of activity in towns and cities. The process of becoming socially intelligent is an important form of learning that we cannot do alone. We become socially intelligent by trial and error in our interactions with others, so that our patient and consistent short-term decisions or actions make us able to act with increased social awareness in both mundane and crisis situations. One of the first steps we can take toward becoming more socially intelligent is to try to understand, or at least recognize, some of the more important complexities and influences in our social conditions, relationships, and history.

When we make a habit of seeing the broader picture of our lives in this way, we automatically consider who we are and what we do in a more realistic daily context, which at the same time amplifies their meanings. As we continue to practice social intelligence in the round of contrasting situations we face routinely, we express our uniqueness more appropriately, we are more likely to achieve our dreams, and we are not unduly influenced by others' expectations. Our increased awareness also enables us to assess both our possibilities and our limitations more accurately.

In order to consider our future directions through using social intelligence, we have to return to the most significant bases of our negotiations with others. These are the bases that have the strongest influence on our social intelligence and on our everyday lives: family, gender, religion, class, culture, and society. When we understand these complex influences more fully, and act with enough knowledge of what keeps us connected to others, we are freer to make SI our own, to pass it on to the next generations, and to deal with the most difficult challenges of the twenty-first century.

X. Making Social Intelligence Our Own

Family

The most important first step in making social intelligence our own is to concentrate on what is going on in at least three generations of our own families. We can only understand the extent to which we are caught up with other family members' pressures and expectations when we examine the dominance of particular patterns of dependency and interaction among as many generations of relatives as possible. To see ourselves as participating members of this most intense emotional system is the beginning of creating the firmest foundation possible for making deliberate use of, and increasing, our social intelligence.

Our most deep-seated postures to life, and our tendencies for repeating some patterns of behavior, result from how we interacted and continue to interact with our parents. Understanding ourselves as a son or a daughter of our parents, whether they are single or married, gives us an important view of who we are, why we want what we want, and what makes us behave the way we do.

It is not enough to see ourselves solely as a son or a daughter, however. We also need to track how we interact with our siblings as a brother or a sister, and how we interact with our grandparents and other family elders. For example, if we are from a large family of siblings, chances are that our lives are qualitatively different from being a member of a small family, or from being an only child or a twin. Patterns of conflict and competition among our siblings, although originally established in our early childhood, still get played out today to some extent. We also carry the imprint of these dependency behaviors with us into other social settings, so that in order to know why we behave the way we do on the job, we need to look closely at what our earliest patterns of interaction were.

Our relationships with our grandparents and other members of our extended kin frequently evolve as a consequence of the intensity of our bonds with our parents. We are emotionally close or distant from our paternal and maternal grandparents to the extent that we are emotionally close or distant from our fathers and mothers. Our dependency on our parents also affects the relationships we build with other members of each of our parents' kin groups, so that we may find that we are incredibly close to our mother's family while at the same time being quite distant from our father's family.

When we understand ourselves more objectively in the broad context of our multiple-generation families, we can begin to see more clearly and more realistically what holds us back from being who we are or who we want to be. With this broader view of ourselves in mind, we can also more clearly discern what we must change in ourselves and in our family bonds if we are to gain more emotional freedom.

However, if we do not look at ourselves in the context of multiple generations, we will continue to have a false or unreliable starting point for whatever else we want to do with our lives. Thinking about ourselves from the perspectives of only one or two generations of our families gives us a fragmented and distorted picture of what is going on in this most important and central of our emotional systems. Such a view means that we get a partial and restricted understanding of who we are and our possibilities for change.

Whatever our intellectual understanding of society, and whether or not we use this intellectual understanding to interpret the world and make enlightened decisions about our behavior, we must come to terms with the power of our family dependencies before we can move into other social spheres effectively. The foundation of social intelligence is thus best built by first knowing who we are in our kin groups. Furthermore, we can only make our most worthwhile contributions to the common good if such a precondition is met. When this crucial step is ignored, we garner losses rather than rewards in our different social enterprises.

Gender

Using social intelligence to understand our families increases our awareness that the gender we learn in our families and in other social contexts has a very strong influence on our behavior. Our sense of being, our thoughts, our attitudes, and our behavior are all patterned according to our gender as well as according to our social class. It is also useful to think about gender as a special kind of social class.

Gender deserves our careful attention because of its obvious visibility in our interactions with others. The visibility of gender, as in the case of race, makes gender count for a great deal in the patterns of interaction we enter into with others, and with regard to the meanings we bestow on these interactions.

X. Making Social Intelligence Our Own

Social intelligence enables us to know how genders are valued differently, and particularly how they have their own distinctive cultural values, economic worth, and social structures. For example, when we consider physiological sexual differences as a distinguishing feature of human beings and social structures, we can consider sex as a determinant of social class, where women usually hold less powerful positions in relation to men.

However, physiological differences may be a superficial and often unreliable way to understand the complexity of gender. First and foremost, gender is a learned cluster of values and behavior rather than a biological given. On the other hand, another crucial determinant of sexual and social behavior, sexual orientation, may not be correlated with learned gender, and may have a physiological source. In sum, gender is extremely complex, and social intelligence can help us to see, unravel, and understand some of these complexities. When we apply SI to discerning how gender influences our own circumstances, we become more socially intelligent and adept.

We make social intelligence our own when we not only understand how and why we operate the way we do in our families, but also when we understand how and why gender plays a major part in our everyday decisions and in our life outcomes. Each life-stage we go through is strongly influenced by our gender expectations, and these are particularly powerful when they are firmly rooted in our families. In fact, we often carry forward not only our own individual gender conditioning in our families, but also that of our same-sex parent. Thus daughters frequently live out the dreams of their mothers, and sons often follow in the footsteps of their fathers. These same-sex gender influences are passed down from generation to generation.

In applying social intelligence to understand our genders, we must first acknowledge the power of our family connections, including three or more generations, in defining the gender expectations we have for ourselves. Then we need to turn to the broader context of our everyday activities, so that we can recognize the many ways in which our attitudes about gender influence whatever we do—from holding a particular body posture, to eating certain foods, and to pursuing specific lifetime goals. In these ways we define our privileges, responsibilities, and limitations through our individual and social understandings of gender.

Gender is also directly related to our economic class positions, and to our racial and ethnic groups. If we are disadvantaged in our class, race, or ethnic group, we will bring social disadvantage rather than social privilege to our gendered situations. We need to see how we are socially burdened and restricted, but in the long run, using social intelligence to understand and change these social intricacies makes us more free and able to define and fulfill our own goals and objectives, in spite of gender and other social limitations. When we make social intelligence our own through the prism of gender, we are able to empower others as well as ourselves.

In doing so, we also realize that we can be more effective in whatever we do when we work with others. Collective action enables us to better the conditions of our own or others' genders, for example, so that gender prejudice and discrimination in society are reduced and minimized. Social intelligence suggests a kind of social justice that appreciates and values the richness in the diversity of gender and gender orientation. Furthermore, this social justice is based on the assumption that freedom for all genders and all gender orientations will increase the common good for all. Thus, when we head in the direction of true gender equality, in all its complex forms, we will be able to build more inclusive and enlightened local and global communities.

Religion

Social intelligence helps us to appreciate religions as tried and tested ways to adapt to harsh or changing physical and social environments. Individuals and societies have used specific religious traditions to guide their behavior from the dawn of civilization; socially scientific sources of guidance pale by comparison. However, some of the more objective ways of viewing religion, aside from the role of the believer, can lead to forms of enlightenment. We need to be both inside religions and outside them in order to benefit from their values in our everyday lives.

Social intelligence shows us that religions are rich and powerful sources of everyday values, ideals, and beliefs throughout history. In fact, some of our most magnificent human accomplishments have been achieved through using religious beliefs as a guide for individual behavior and community change.

X. Making Social Intelligence Our Own

We are influenced in whatever we do by our values, ideals, and beliefs. Consequently, understanding religious and secular influences in our individual lives and in society helps us to see who we believe we are, why we have particular ideals, and what goals we think are important. When we use social intelligence to assess the significance of the interplay and conflict among religious and secular values, we will know ourselves better, and will ultimately be more effective in our accomplishments.

Religious influences do not descend from the heavens, or reach us through any particularly extraordinary or supernatural means. By contrast we are socialized into our specific religious beliefs, usually through our families, often at very early ages. Therefore the patterns of dominance, or of religious leadership, in our families are important to scrutinize when we use our social intelligence to clarify our understanding of the source of our religious and secular beliefs.

If we want to change our religious beliefs, especially as an outcome of seeing them for what they are in terms of our family or social relationships, we have to make deliberate efforts to reorganize our values and to act according to our new priorities. If we do nothing about the beliefs we have already internalized, we will continue to automatically set out from these already-established bases in our daily behavior.

Each traditional religion or denomination has its own characteristic hierarchy of values. We may choose to accept a cluster of traditional religious values, or we may reject this time-tested ordering of values. We may also modify our traditional religious belief systems by espousing additional secular or contemporary values, so that we make the traditional religious belief systems work better for us in contemporary society.

When we make this new kind of synthesis of sacred and secular values, we do not disrespect religion, nor do we play God by creating our own religions. Rather, reordering our values is a useful and viable way to accommodate traditional beliefs that do not seem to work well in contemporary society. When we create our own syntheses of sacred and secular beliefs we are frequently better able to adapt to current circumstances, and to introduce changes that enhance the common good.

As we progress, through trial and error, in establishing our new priorities or different values in our daily lives, we may increase our religiosity rather than secularize our values. Social intelligence suggests that we have many choices to make, especially about which values we want to espouse; the significance of making our value choices carefully and deliberately is that they will then be more likely to become our own. If we automatically internalize ready-made creeds and dogmas, there is a greater probability that we will behave blindly rather than with a high level of awareness about our needs and the needs of others. Mixing and matching religious and secular beliefs does not mean that we turn our backs on traditional religions, but rather that we deliberately broaden our horizons to include those beliefs which are congruent from other traditions.

Broadening our world views does not necessarily result in decreasing the importance of religion in our individual lives or in society. Instead, when we expand our world views, we also enhance and invigorate both our religious and secular beliefs, so that they become more meaningful bases for our conduct and contributions to others. When we use social intelligence in this manner to claim our values, we become more socially intelligent in our transactions with others, and more effective in accomplishing our goals.

Class

In order to make social intelligence our own, we need to see and understand why social class plays a major part in influencing who we are and what we desire with our lives. Social class can be thought of as having an economic base, or being more directly related to particular characteristics we have, such as race, ethnicity, age, gender, religion, or physical strength. Social class may also be a direct reflection of our special interests, or the degree of social honor we claim or have. In sum, social class is the group with which we identify and feel to belong, or with which others identify us.

Our personal identities, as well as our social identities, are usually closely connected to whichever group or groups we believe are the most meaningful to us. At the same time that we struggle to create authentic individual and social identities, however, others tend to objectify us by associating us with groups of their choosing. For example, some may focus on a particular physical trait we have, like race or sex, as being more important than those characteristics which we consider to be significant.

X. Making Social Intelligence Our Own

The sources of our social class placements are not of paramount importance, whether we identify ourselves as members of a particular social class or others do so. However, it is only when we know how we and others associate groups or classes with us that we can free ourselves from social class expectations, and become more socially intelligent. Social intelligence is the capacity to see our social class memberships, and to modify the influence such memberships have on our behavior. Furthermore, we make social intelligence our own when we try to accomplish these difficult and challenging tasks.

One of the complexities involved in understanding how social classes influence our everyday behavior is that each one of us is simultaneously a member of several social classes. Our different social class memberships overlap, largely because we all have some economic resources, racial characteristics, ethnicity, ages, sexual characteristics, physical abilities, and special interests, which are valued and honored in contrasting ways by ourselves and by others.

Therefore, in making social intelligence our own, we need to assess which of our particular social classes are the most important to us, and which ones appear to be the most powerful determinants in our lives from the points of view of others. The strength and influence of our social class associations and affiliations will inevitably change over time, during our lifetimes as well as throughout history. However, we get a head start in claiming social intelligence when we try to assess what the influences of our social classes are in our immediate past and current situations.

One of the most significant advantages of understanding the complexity of class structures, and their impacts on our opportunities, is that we become more autonomous. This means that making social intelligence our own, with respect to our social classes, enables us to be less trapped in our own or others' social class expectations. However, unless we actively continue to struggle to make social intelligence our own, we may quickly lose sight of how powerful social class influences can be. Increasing our social intelligence is both important and beneficial because we need to be guided by our own thoughts at all times, rather than to be subjected to the dominance of other individuals and groups.

We transcend our social class influences more successfully when we understand them for what they are, and deliberately choose to rely more on social intelligence to guide us through our everyday activities than social class influences. However, SI alerts us to the need to keep some awareness of what others expect of us with regard to our social classes, so that we can conform to social norms when it is in our interests to do so, or deviate when we think this is best. We are stronger individuals and contributors to communities when we are our own persons rather than when we strive to accommodate social class influences.

Culture

Social intelligence shows us that culture permeates everything we learn, think, and do. We are, in fact, creatures of culture, and it is this cultural heritage and base of civilization that distinguishes us from other mammals.

One aspect of our shared human and social predicament is that we internalize values, beliefs, ideals, and other aspects of culture without really being aware that we are doing so. We automatically breathe in the cultures to which we are exposed, so that unless we make deliberate efforts to shape this process of learning different values, we are extremely vulnerable to the imperiousness of these external influences.

In order to make social intelligence our own, we must consistently be selective in our choices about our ongoing cultural experiences. When we exercise our freedom to choose the cultural influences to which we are subjected, we become correspondingly more in control of what and how we learn. Our ongoing series of opportunities to make deliberate choices about cultural influences means that we may decide to pursue formal education programs, or to associate with specific groups that hold a certain interest for us. We may also opt to be more discriminating about our various leisure pursuits or the many ways in which we decide how to spend our time and energy. If we conduct our everyday lives along these lines we increase our social intelligence and at the same time make it more truly our own.

Knowing what the most significant values are in our mainstream society is an effective starting point for filtering out unwanted cultural influences. We can use a follow-up method of substitution to move us along in this process. In principle, we substitute what we desire for what we reject in relation to cultural influences. We make decisions to at least cut out those cultural

X. Making Social Intelligence Our Own

experiences that we do not want to have, partly in order to become more open to the kinds of cultural experiences we really wish to have. When we are not sure what kind of values, beliefs, or ideals we want, we may be much clearer about what we do not want. In this respect, an initial stage of the elimination of what we think are less desirable cultural influences can be both helpful and beneficial in our quest to make our social intelligence our own.

Another way to be more coherent about our cultural choices, and to be able to make more consistent decisions about what we will and will not do, is to characterize the broad scope of our cultural possibilities as demonstrating particular patterns. For example, we might think of culture as being traditional or modern, or as being individual- or collective-oriented, or as being constructive or destructive. These three dualities reflect an existing tension between the three sets of extreme clusters of values, so that it is easier for us to situate ourselves closer to one or the other end of these polar opposites. These structures or continua can also serve as a kind of starting point for understanding where we are in relation to others' values, beliefs, and ideals.

In order to increase our social intelligence, and to make it our own, we need to find some workable ways to modify our own socialization, or at least to recognize the power of cultural influences within the processes of our own socialization. Even though we may decide to keep the values, beliefs, and ideals we already have, we may still be able to scrutinize our own behavior sufficiently so that we find more viable ways to increase the impact of our values in our everyday lives. When we go through such a process of self examination within different social contexts we predictably increase our social intelligence and understand more fully how we can be more effective in communicating those values, beliefs, and ideals which mean the most to us.

Culture is made up of symbolic, meaningful reflections of how we live and what we accomplish. Social intelligence enables us to critically assess whether we are really doing what we think we are doing, and to what extent our actions will have a long-term constructive or destructive impact on others. It may be more comfortable to think that whatever we do does not count for much, but SI gives us the capacity to acknowledge that our actions do make a difference, even though we are mere individuals struggling to survive in the complex morass of culture and society.

Society

We make social intelligence our own by analyzing the quality and characteristics of our participation in different levels of social complexity in our everyday lives. Although each level of social complexity has its own kind of power and influence in defining who we are and what we do, understanding ourselves is deeper and more effective when we consider family, gender, religion, class, culture and society as an ever-expanding sequence of social influences in our lives.

Thus seeing and examining ourselves in broad social perspectives are vital dimensions of making social intelligence our own. We cannot know who we are, or what we can effectively do with our lives, without seriously considering ourselves in relation to our societies and the global community. This form of broad social context gives us meaning, purpose, and direction, as well as helps us to understand more fully who we are in relation to others in society and in the global community. Once we grasp the power and significance of the holistic "in relation" aspect of our being, thinking, and doing, we increase the possibility that we will become more truly autonomous, and at the same time better able to exercise our agency within complex social realities and social change processes.

Societies and the global community have lives of their own. These vast social networks are more than the sum of their parts, with the result that their individual members are relatively powerless as well as dependent on these larger groupings for their survival and well-being. Although we may not recognize, or want to admit, these crude but basic characteristics of our relationships with our societies and with the global community, our powerlessness and dependencies are very real. Social intelligence helps us to acknowledge such bottom-line facts of our existence, so that we can build on our essential human frailties and eventually strengthen our abilities to take charge of our destinies. When we make social intelligence our own, by deliberately nurturing the habit of seeing ourselves within the broad perspectives of our societies and the world, we will be able to move forward with our everyday lives more freely.

Some of the most significant aspects of our relationships to society include political systems and historical conditions. We are subjected to the rule of law within different kinds of political systems, and we are inevitably and simultaneously pushed and pulled by the currents of history. It matters a great deal that we at least believe that we have some degree of influence on established political processes, and that we understand that we need to have at least minimum levels of peace and security in order to survive and thrive. Some of our most harsh social conditions, which may lead to the annihilation of individuals and whole societies, are caused by inequities in political power and widespread war. These kinds of political imbalances and violence can bring about the demise of civilizations as well as of individuals and societies.

Social intelligence, when used thoughtfully by political leaders, has the potential to make the world a better place for all. SI is also a useful resource for the most oppressed. The kinds of awareness, knowledge, and perspective which derive from social intelligence can help individuals and groups to transcend even the harshest social conditions, because it serves as a guide for them to think more clearly about what must be done in order to survive and thrive. Although SI may be abused by those in power, and may become a means to achieve destructive ends, it can also be a decisive, constructive force for increasing the common good, and for attending to and meeting all kinds of human needs.

In the final analysis, one of the main effects of making social intelligence our own is to become historical actors. We make our greatest contributions to society when we have a clear sense of what is truly significant in our contemporary times, and why current conditions are in creative tension with the past and the future. Making constructive use of social intelligence is a disciplined and anchored way for us to act meaningfully within and through the social underpinnings of history, by calling into play our more sophisticated understanding of political pressures. We are effective historical actors when we maintain our freedom and autonomy in spite of existing political pressures, and when we achieve goals that increase the common good of society and the global community.

XI. Passing
Social Intelligence On

A lthough we may not give much thought to the possibility and importance of passing social intelligence on to others, there is a direct relationship between how socially intelligent we can continue to be and the extent to which we give it away to others. Social intelligence is a way to survive, a foundation for civilization, and a hope for the future. However, these ideals can only be met when we deliberately make provisions for continuities in handing down this vital information.

Thus, in order to keep social intelligence once we have made it our own, we must make special efforts to give it away to whoever wants to learn it, and most especially to members of the younger generations. Unless we pass this kind of strategic information on to others, we run the risk of losing its benefits, and of losing the increased social intelligence we built and thought was our own.

Because social intelligence has emotional as well as rational roots, it must take hold deeply in our being in order for it to inspire us and to make optimal changes in our lives. For example, we become more socially intelligent through patient, consistent short-term decisions and actions, as well as by acting with social awareness in crisis situations. Thus we pass it on in both rational and emotional circumstances through our everyday routines, and through acting responsibly in compelling dilemmas.

Social intelligence is a grounded way to see and estimate the major influences in our social realities, and it is also a way to amplify the possibilities for meaning in our lives. In these respects social intelligence helps us, as well as others, to see ourselves for who we are, and at the same time to see increased options for deepening meaning in our lives. When we practice social intelligence by giving it away, we express our uniqueness in different ways, and we make it more likely that we achieve and pass on our most cherished dreams. Our successes from these endeavors result from our firm footing in social reality, which gives us sufficient strength to resist any inclination to do merely what others expect of us.

Like anything else we accomplish from deep learning, we want to pass our social intelligence on to the next generation. Our experiences, trials, and errors move us forward, so that when we depend more on social intelligence, we act with increased faith and perseverance. Our personal efforts to live successfully through faith and perseverance show that putting these eternal values into action yields benefits for all. Thus we inspire the next generation most when our own lives are inspiring to us.

When we try to communicate what we have learned about social intelligence to others, we automatically increase the common good. When we get more people in society interested in increasing and applying SI, the shared pool of good deeds and useful information expands. In this way our actions, not our words, are the clearest and most enduring message of social intelligence, and they lead us on toward real achievement.

The values and ideals of social intelligence grow through multiplying apprenticeships, mentors, public education, and empathetic personal communications. This beneficial sharing is a result of a realization that social intelligence is not the intellectual property of elites, but rather a series of social principles upon which we can depend each day. The principles of SI can carry us forward, and those who try to learn and use it will be moved to act constructively in the great unknown.

The arenas in which we pass SI on to others should be the most vital social sources of social intelligence: family, gender, religion, class, culture, and society. This is because the foundations of social intelligence need to be as strong and as enduring as possible, and this is best accomplished by moving through these different zones. We not only make social intelligence our own in these particular areas of social interaction, but we also pass it on to others in the most meaningful ways possible. As we give it away, we ourselves grow stronger, and the cycle of giving is started again.

XI. Passing Social Intelligence On

Family

Our families are the original sources and emotional hot spots of our conditioning, and of the stances we habitually assume toward life and the world. In a very unequivocal sense, our family dependencies are a strong and persistent influence in how we deal with self and society. In these respects our families are our first experiences of social realities, and of the interplay between social intelligence and these social realities.

We make social intelligence our own when we express our deliberately chosen values in the emotionally challenging arena of our families. By extension, it is important for us to give back to this group, which can consist largely of passing SI on to diverse family members. These exchanges need not be artificially contrived or formally presented. Simply setting an example of how we lead our own lives is a sufficiently vital message to pass on to other family members.

Our first experiences building a resource and a reserve of social intelligence frequently derive from the experiences and observations of intergenerational exchanges. At the beginning of our lives, we are very much on the receiving end of particular ideas and information, and as we mature we understand that we can learn at first hand what the passage of time really means when we talk to our elders. Family history is usually the first kind of history we learn, and situating ourselves in this stream of information and social connections is an important part of becoming an adult.

Even when we reach maturity, we need to continue to grow within our family arenas. We can best observe who we are when we scrutinize our relationships with other family members. This is because our deepest feelings and emotions are evoked by these particular significant others. Part of attaining maturity includes assuming the responsibility to pass on whatever we have learned to the next generation. Although this exchange occurs most obviously when we become parents, making a transition to parenthood is not a necessary condition for expressing the need to give to the next generation. Many other kinds of teaching-learning exchanges occur in family contexts.

Living in reasonably close emotional proximity to our families—which means that we build meaningful relationships with our relatives as best we can—enables us to see the shared family biases and tendencies to repeat certain attitudes and patterns of behavior among the different generations. Most important is the intensity of the pressure that members of the same family feel from other relatives to conform rather than be different.

Social intelligence helps us to untangle the most pernicious effects of these powerful complexities of interdependence, which run between generations as well as among members of the same generation. When we increase our social intelligence, we become more autonomous, and therefore freer of a particular family's pressures to conform. It is only when we achieve this beneficial position of autonomy and freedom, with respect to our families, that we are most able to give to other relatives, especially to those who are younger.

Social intelligence can also guide us about what it is that we might communicate to our relatives, including elderly family members as well as the youngest members of our families. First and foremost, we need to pass on everyday survival skills and basic social skills. We frequently accomplish this by telling stories about members of our families. As we do this we can help our older relatives, and even deceased family members, to play significant parts in the important task of building and maintaining a family history. Even though most family histories are replete with questionable anecdotes about deceased and living relatives rather than facts, this is always a vital way to teach all family members about their social heritage. Oral family histories fascinate both young and old, and family photographs can make past family events come alive and seem more personal. During these kinds of exchanges, family members necessarily become more objective about their current emotional and behavioral situations. For example, relatives can be a little more detached from present family crises when they know more about what went on in the past in their families.

Another way to pass social intelligence on within our families is to make sure that we maintain meaningful contact with as many relatives as possible in our entire kin systems. This kind of deliberate networking within the different generations of our families allows us to have a wide variety of interpersonal exchanges, which frequently evoke strong feelings. If our relatives are estranged from us, or from other members of our families, these situations can challenge us to bridge the emotional gaps. In addition, when relatives are in active conflict with each other, we can seize opportunities to temper some of the hard feelings expressed, perhaps serving as a mediator.

XI. Passing Social Intelligence On

Whatever we decide to do in our broad kin networks, merely existing within our families inevitably creates many opportunities to pass on social intelligence. Interacting with our relatives, whatever the nature of these communications, increases our own social intelligence and gives it away to those people most important to us, even in spite of ourselves.

Gender

Social intelligence confirms that gender is partly a product of family conditioning, and partly a result of sexual controls and social arrangements in a particular society and throughout the world. Gender is one of the most primitive and most basic criteria for categorizing people, and polarizations between the two gender types of male and female are powerful, widespread influences. Even though there are many variations in physiological sexual characteristics, sexual orientations, transgender presentations, and sex changes in contemporary society, many people are still strongly affected by customs and institutions that regulate sexual behavior in order to meet the usually dominant heterosexual ideals.

Gender awareness is an important component of social intelligence. One way to make it our own is to experiment by behaving in ways that run counter to others' gender expectations for us. Also, we increase our social intelligence when we enter into informing or learning exchanges with those who are not aware of the gender nuances and gender power imbalances in our everyday social exchanges.

Thus we increase our SI when we go about our everyday routines with a heightened gender consciousness. Others can often follow the example we give through our behavior more easily than when we merely talk about the gender wisdom we have accumulated. One way to make a beginning in passing on social intelligence about gender is to act autonomously in our families whatever our gender may be. To the extent that we manage to deviate successfully from our families' gender expectations for us, we demonstrate courage, strength, and social intelligence. This model encourages other family members to follow suit.

Because, historically, women have been discriminated against more than men, it is imperative for women to be able to learn from other women about the strengths and weaknesses of conventional gender socialization, and about the hierarchies of gender power that encompass them. When we enter into this kind of exchange about socially intelligent survival skills, we become more secure in our own selves, and we are less negatively influenced or restricted by our family gender socialization.

Similarly, men can learn a great deal from sharing their social intelligence about male conditioning and patriarchies with other men, especially among family members. Some families control men's behavior and ideals to such a great extent that men find it extremely difficult to express their feelings or to be autonomous. However, whatever gender influences men have experienced, their social intelligence will increase when they pass on their most enlightened knowledge about gender to others.

Gender influences in families and society are truly pervasive. We usually get out of bed in the morning breathing like a man or a woman, and then we set about our daily tasks continuing to act as a man or a woman. The social expectations for men and women are often complementary or polarized, and we establish two different cultural and moral orders for men and women as we interact with each other. Unless we use social intelligence to see these influences on our behavior clearly, we will be subjected to the rigors of gender controls in whatever we think or do. Gender liberation begins in our minds, and this important freedom is then expressed in our behavior.

One of the most enduring ways to pass gender wisdom on to the next generation is to communicate with children. As well as imitating us, which is a powerful influence, even small children can engage meaningfully in conversations about what it means to be a boy or girl, a man or woman. They are fascinated with the differences they observe, and unfortunately they frequently pick up the most conservative ideas about what is right and proper for them to do when they conform to gender expectations. Limiting children's exposure to harmful gender stereotypes when they are very young may be a satisfactory way to communicate healthier ideas about gender to the next generation. However, sooner or later, children will have to deal with a culture that is saturated with sexuality and false gender messages. Hence some people believe that it may be best to ease children into the deep end of this experience when they are very young.

All in all, speaking with children frankly and openly about sex and gender is consistently helpful to them and to the adults involved. These forms of thoughtful communications are much needed in our world of conflicted gender messages. To the extent that we can encourage children to be critical of the gender roles assigned to them by others, we help them to mature and to become stronger in themselves.

Religion

Social intelligence provides us with an important overview of the basic foundational importance of religion in society and in our personal lives. We cannot benefit from denying the significance of religion in the world, even though we may not consider ourselves to be religious. The social realities of religions transcend individuals, cultures, and particular societies.

Social intelligence shows us that for many people religion is passed from generation to generation within their families. This means that our personal and emotional development is frequently tied closely to our religious socialization; what we believe and practice with regard to religion often imitates, or at least reflects, our family relationships. When religious zeal is the most salient characteristic of the emotional content of a family's messages about religion, for example, individual family members may rebel and move away from the behavior patterns of their relatives, going in what appear to be completely different directions. However, this kind of rebellious response is essentially formulated in opposition to the family rather than independently of the family. These rebellious family members are still intimately tied to the emotional systems of their families in spite of their desires to break free of them.

Social intelligence also reminds us that family dynamics, such as dominance, come into play in the transmission of shared family definitions of religion and their customary religious practices. When we are children we tend to conform, in order to survive, to whatever the patterns of dominance and leadership are in our families, including agreeing to participate in particular shared religious experiences. It is only when we make our religious beliefs and practices truly our own that we can resist the pressures of other family members to follow their wishes about our religious observances.

In families that have professional religious leaders among their members, these contrasting patterns of emotional dependency and individual autonomy in religious beliefs and practices frequently occur in more marked ways. Because we are unable to control how anyone else thinks and acts in the long run, we need to stay aware that the emotional underpinnings of religious practices in all families reflect family dependencies. We do not become religious in a vacuum, or usually by divine revelation, so we often have to cut through our many strong feelings and false assumptions about others and the world before we can be truly autonomous in our religious behavior.

One liberating aspect of gaining autonomy in our religious beliefs is to develop our capacities to tell others of the trials and tribulations we have dealt with as we came to formulate our most cherished religious values. It is also liberating to let others know what we value most about being religious or not being religious. Many people, old as well as young, can benefit from frank and open conversations about our deepest beliefs, because this kind of exchange is particularly helpful in the difficult and challenging process of formulating our own most significant views and values.

Social intelligence reminds us that we thrive most when we relate, in some meaningful way, to religious institutions in society. In passing SI on to others, we merely need to describe our own experiences to others, rather than try to persuade them to see themselves and the world in the same ways that we do. Religion in society is a powerful force, and we must stay alert and ready for the possible infiltration of this influence in our everyday lives. It is only when we are socially intelligent about religion, and participate in ongoing dialogues with others about our most cherished beliefs, that we can be fully aware of the power and pervasiveness of this influence in our families, friendships, society, and the global community.

Passing on social intelligence about religion helps us to sustain our awareness about the daily importance of religious and secular values, and completes the cycle of reciprocity with regard to religious socialization. In passing religious social intelligence on, we may also be inspired to participate more fully in social changes. We may be more motivated and empowered by our continuously maturing religious values to take action to counter social injustices in society, for example. We may also be more motivated to face the future realistically, with our strengthened religious beliefs, especially as we concurrently make the effort to pass our most sacred values on as an integral part of our social intelligence.

XI. Passing Social Intelligence On

Class

Social intelligence shows us that class—whether based on economic or other shared characteristics—is a significant dimension of social conditions and life outcomes. We organize power relations and social status along class lines, and some kinds of social change are triggered by class conflicts. Thus when we make social intelligence our own, and pass it on to others, we must become increasingly aware of the myriad ways in which class affects our behavior, as well as the behavior of those around us, including members of the international community.

In some respects class divides us in very basic ways into the haves and have-nots, and our world views may become polarized by this overly simplistic perspective. However, we may choose to deliberately support the underdog while being a member of an upper class, and we may also opt out of the competitiveness among classes, or out of the striving to keep up with the Joneses. Social intelligence reminds us that whatever we choose to do, class is an important social reality, which we cannot afford to deny or ignore. It also shows us that class has the capacity to transform lives, because it may either limit or expand class members' opportunities and life chances.

Part of making social intelligence our own includes acknowledging our different class memberships. We may belong to several classes based on economic resources, gender, sexual orientation, race, ethnicity, religion, or able-bodiedness. As we recognize which classes are most salient in our lives, we also need to assess where we stand in relation to mainstream society and other classes. When we pass social intelligence about class on to others, we automatically heighten our awareness of classes. This enables us to draw attention to the many ways in which our own classes and their relationships with each other impinge on what we do and on how we think about ourselves.

When we speak to individuals of any age, we may be impressed that they have little or no acknowledged awareness of the difference that class makes to their daily lives. People may be happy to describe their lives, but usually very few see themselves clearly in relation to their own economic class or other kinds of classes. In this respect they have very little class-consciousness.

Although we could conclude that not being aware of our classes is free of immediate penalties, it is particularly in the long run that the pernicious effects of class prejudices and discrimination limit what we can do and even feel. Although we may not know it, we are often trapped by class expectations, and we can only release ourselves from these limiting influences when we learn more about the social complexities of classes through our everyday behavior.

Passing social intelligence about classes on to others is one step in a direction that will ultimately increase options and further progress toward liberation, equality, and freedom. When we know who the social enemies are in our lives, we can avoid or defeat them and get on track more easily.

Even though not everybody gains freedom from merely knowing about the existence of their classes, at least we can begin to see and understand more fully what being a member of a lower class means for the quality of our life experiences. We are more likely to have empathy for others when we are not oblivious to their restrictions and suffering. This means that although passing social intelligence about class on will predictably heighten our own and others' awareness about social class, one outcome may be to increase empathy rather than to make moves to change the social hierarchies in which we participate on a daily basis.

In the best of all worlds, passing social intelligence about class on to others will increase changes in class systems, and will make social stratification more humane rather than rigid and punitive. We will break out of class extremes and polarities, however, only when we understand that it is vitally necessary to resolve problems related to poverty and other kinds of harsh social realities. For example, social intelligence enables us to see and identify some of the negative social consequences that flow from the sheer abundance and excesses that exist in some societies throughout the world.

Culture

In many ways we do not have a choice about whether or not we will pass culture on. At all times and in all places we transmit values, beliefs, and ideals to others in spite of ourselves. What is at issue is whether we become more deliberate about how we present ourselves in everyday life. We also need to ask ourselves whether we want to make a special effort to communicate our social intelligence about culture to others. SI helps us to determine what important aspects of our cultures we think we need to pass on for the survival of future generations and the world.

XI. Passing Social Intelligence On

We may pass culture on indiscriminately to others, or we may choose rational or irrational ways to transmit our values, beliefs, and ideals. Whatever we do, we pass culture on to others because we cannot live without making symbolic communications. Meaning is an integral part of social gestures, and we must interact with others in order to survive.

When we use social intelligence to guide our actions, we may decide what we will do according to what makes the most sense to us, or what feels right. Although either of these bases of decision-making can follow tradition for tradition's sake, or our strongest feelings and hunches, we remain more in control of our actions when we use reason to make our choices. We become freer when we are aware of the choices we make and can make.

Passing social intelligence about culture on to others comes in different forms. We may pass on information and facts about different racial or ethnic heritages, or we may encourage members of younger generations to pursue education or a particular course of career development. When we make these choices about what aspect of our own culture we want to pass on to others, we become more aware of the many diverse aspects of our own cultural heritages.

Because cultures may be traditional or modern, we need to be aware of whether we are passing on old, established ways of doing things, or newer, innovative modes created by conditions in contemporary society. There is a danger that if we look too far into the past for our answers, these models will not relate well to current circumstances. It is imperative that we stay alert to how viable our ideas, values, and beliefs are for present situations. Although social traditions are time-tested, we need some degree of flexibility in our social communications and social arrangements if we are to thrive well into the future.

Cultures may also be oriented toward individuals or toward a collective, common good. We have to make a moral decision about whether we support self-interest as an optimal way of being, or whether we enter into a quest to find new ways to expand the common good. Ultimately this means that each of us has a responsibility to examine the long-range consequences and implications of our behavior. In doing this, we need to assess whether we are moving toward perpetuating self-interest as an organizing principle of culture, or bringing about a culture based on social solidarity and shared benefits. Such an awareness of our own cultural contributions makes it easier for us to be rationally selective when we pass social intelligence about culture on to others.

Another basic choice in passing social intelligence about culture on is whether we will perpetuate constructive or destructive values and beliefs. We need to ask ourselves, for example, how we can promote values and social structures that increase empathy and compassion. We also need to know whether we can find ways to decrease values and social structures that lead to alienation and hatred.

When we pass social intelligence about culture on to others we must be aware of how all our interactions are messages in their own right. We have to become living examples of the cultures we want to bring into the present as well as the future world. It is only when we know what we are doing in this respect that we will be able to be heard for what we actually say when we speak about our own experiences. We cannot have an impact or influence on others when we do not know what we are about.

Society

We pass social intelligence about society on to others in many ways, whether we are aware of doing so or not. One of these is through travel to a foreign country. Being immersed in the daily give and take of different customs and languages brings the kind of culture shock that enhances our capacities to be objective about society. When we are in the contrasting setting of a foreign country we see and experience quite sharply the limitations and ethnocentricity of our world-views; at the same time we increase our understanding of how societies differ from each other in deep and complex ways.

Taking younger family members with us when we travel to foreign countries is a particularly good opportunity to pass social intelligence about society on to them. We can enter into lively exchanges about the contrasting influences different societies have on our lives more easily when we are living abroad than when we stay on home territory. We can also sustain and encourage international friendships and continued contacts to extend this beneficial learning experience about the impact of society on our everyday life.

XI. Passing Social Intelligence On

Transmitting the habit of putting our lives in a broader perspective is another way of passing the benefits of cultivating social intelligence about society on to others. We need to see the broader picture of events in our lives if we are to understand our own situations fully. Also, SI shows us that we can encourage others to embrace such a breadth of vision more successfully in those times when they are trying to cope with particular incidents or even crises in their daily lives. Even if the issues discussed seem to be personal, like depressed feelings or a sense of being exploited by others, there are many ways in which these personal matters can be linked to broader forces in society. Putting our problems in a social perspective or context is a sound way to sum up our situations more objectively and more meaningfully. This message is heard more readily when it is used to actually reduce social pressures felt in a particular period of time.

Encouraging younger people to discuss or participate in politics is another way to broaden their visions about what is going on in society and what they can do about it. In this respect it is again very important to set an example of what an involved citizen does for society, and even for the international community. We do not live in a vacuum, and we have multiple responsibilities to others, especially to those who are less fortunate than we are. When we live according to socially intelligent priorities, and express our deliberately chosen values in whatever we do, we automatically pass these skills on to other people.

Society is evolving in history. We can describe and discuss these perspectives in order to demonstrate the usefulness of these views, and to deepen the understanding that we are all actors in complex change processes whether or not we precipitate—or think that we precipitate—the changes we experience. Even when we respond passively to historical events, this does not mean that social changes do not affect us.

Knowing that we are historical actors inspires others to consider these responsibilities. Being a historical actor means that in order to give back to society we must stay ready to respond in ways that are called for and clearly needed. In addition, we need to be aware of what is going on in society and in the world in order to act in historically informed ways. Reacting solely to our own self-interest is not enough, and it is not a socially intelligent way to be in the long run.

It is difficult to be an actor in evolution because this time frame is so much broader and more difficult to understand than what we define as history. However, we need to know how human beings have evolved, and to what extent their behavior is influenced by the environment, if we are to be socially intelligent and in a sufficiently strong position to pass on this knowledge to others. For example, we need to be aware that our emotional being is powerful, and that our emotional intelligence is one component of social intelligence. Being more astute about understanding human nature and potential will make us more effective participants in the future.

XII. Social Intelligence and the Twenty-First Century

It is often said that making any predictions about the future is unprofessional and even foolhardy. However, being prepared for different contingencies, being flexible and open-minded in designing effective strategies, and being idealistic, yet realistic, in our visions of possibilities seem to be sensible goals to have in order to work toward increasing possibilities for a better future.

Social intelligence is a source of designs and strategies for creating new kinds of community and for living peacefully in these contemporary times of social reorganization, revolutionary technology, globalization, and terrorism. Our worlds have changed in substance and size during the last few decades. For example, increased contacts among different races and diverse ethnic groups point up some of the inadequacies of traditional ways of doing things. As a result, we can perhaps agree that we need socially intelligent imaginations to pull us out of the complex problems and crises that already face us at the beginning of the twenty-first century.

Social intelligence can be used as a guide to improve how we do things and how we can coexist more peacefully with increased social justice. When we reduce inequalities we are more inclusive, we have a fuller appreciation of diversity, and we can cooperate more fully. These kinds of social conditions enable us to increase the openness of our communications within our societies and in our international relations, so that we can build more viable social structures to actually meet our shared needs.

Social intelligence can be thought of as a means, or a tool, to help create visions and design strategies that will improve our most harsh and most restrictive social conditions. It is only by having such a breadth of vision, which derives directly from using SI, that we can realistically aim to benefit all. This is because social intelligence is rooted in informed assumptions about the ultimate oneness of the world community, as well as the powerful deep-seated nature of the social realities, relations, and complexities that we experience on a daily basis.

By contrast, when we do not deliberately access social intelligence, we produce only limited plans and establish relatively unenlightened leadership, which will inevitably intensify and aggravate both longstanding and current social problems. However, if we decide to change these ways of doing things by using social intelligence to guide our future actions, we will be better able to integrate emotion, feeling, and reason in thoughtful strategies and interventions. This means that social intelligence can play a crucial role in creating the best possible world for all.

One of social intelligence's strengths is that it provides holistic perspectives on past, current, and future social conditions. When we use social intelligence, we can understand the social context of history, and appreciate the importance of keeping a continuous focus on the broader picture of our immediate situations. A reliable way to sustain this breadth of vision is to consider and then assess the power of the impact of several significant dimensions of society as simultaneously as possible. These particularly influential social junctures are family, gender, religion, class, culture, and society. Because these points of connection with others are often involuntary, as well as more or less universal throughout time and space, understanding them informs us about related social complexities in small groups and the global community, including our relationships to them. Consequently, the social intelligence derived from these observations, reflections, and applications improves our abilities to navigate our lives on a daily basis and to look ahead to the twenty-first century.

Therefore, although we cannot predict the future, at least we can be more prepared for it; we can make deliberate use of our social intelligence to increase our collective state of readiness. Through rich educational experiences, as well as other kinds of effective learning processes, we can limit some of the predictable social hazards that are inevitably promoted by ignorance, and we can concurrently develop human potential more responsibly.

XII. Social Intelligence and the Twenty-First Century

Social intelligence gives us a reliable foundation for our optimism about our life chances in the future, especially if we work consistently toward increasing social justice and building new kinds of more empathetic communities.

Family

One of the ways in which social intelligence can help us to respond constructively to social conditions of the twenty-first century is to be able to appreciate, and to know the social implications of the necessary ongoing changes that are taking place in our families. Increased diversity, widespread geographical mobility, world wide political migrations, and shifting patterns of intergenerational exchanges in families make today's families different from families in the twentieth century. There is an unavoidable and continuing need to adapt to broad changes that are taking place in our societies and in the international community. Thus it is imperative that our families develop new ways of doing things rather than rely on traditional forms and processes that do not fit well with contemporary circumstances.

Trends in our families are, in fact, a barometer of change itself. Even though families tend to influence society in conservative ways, meaning that they do not change substantially over long periods of time, they must eventually accommodate other kinds of social changes if they are to survive and continue into the future. However, social intelligence reminds us that given this basic need for families to adapt to society, we also need to have a certain degree of family solidarity within societies if we are to be able to procreate and rear young generations successfully.

When we can accept the fact that families come in many shapes and sizes, exhibiting a wide range of patterns of behavior, we will be able to work toward establishing flexibility and tenacity as signs of family strength. However, in order to move to this level of understanding, we must let go of antiquated ideas of family traditions, which can do little more than perpetuate hierarchical relationships and rigid ways of doing things. Social intelligence shows us that we must not go back to the past in our search for viable family ideals in the twenty-first century, because they cannot serve us well either today or in the future.

Social Intelligence in Everyday Life

Our strongest families maintain meaningful ties with their local communities; they consequently form a strong foundation for many different forms of relationships and social groups. If we are interested in an improved future for society, we must become more invested in creating a stronger future for our families. This does not mean that we merely need to form our own families through a need or desire to procreate, but rather that we must also stay connected to members of the older generations of our families. When we nourish and sustain our roots from the past in this way, we are more able to move into the future with strength, creativity, and purpose.

Letting go of our deepest interpersonal expectations for family roles—for example, spouse, mother, father, brother, sister, or cousin—also increases the flexibility of our families, and makes them sufficiently elastic to be able to withstand more of the severe stresses of everyday life. We cannot afford to be unrealistic in our current and future visions of our families if they are to be viable for the twenty-first century.

Families are one of the most influential microcosms of society and the international community, and they also reflect the quality of the everyday life of particular communities or societies. How we treat our children and our elderly relatives largely represents to what extent a society is empathetic or compassionate. In a very real way we are our families and they are the fabric of society. The reciprocity between individuals and their families links us to social conditions in the past, present, and future, and if we want to use social intelligence to build a better future, we have to create stronger families now.

One of the most important principles in using social intelligence to create more viable families is to loosen up family bonds. We must be loyal and responsible with regard to meeting our families' needs, but we also need to participate as citizens of the world, by developing some clearly defined, meaningful roles. We cannot bring children into the world only to honor our families because the problems and work of the twenty-first century are so complex and demanding that we need all the help we can find. Thus we must balance our goals to increase our family strengths with nurturing and realizing our shared mission to build a stronger, more just society for the twenty-first century.

XII. Social Intelligence and the Twenty-First Century

Gender

Social intelligence shows us that gender is a vitally significant part of family life, and is also a globally accepted base for many different kinds of institutional and social arrangements. Social intelligence demonstrates that gender is learned behavior, and is therefore essentially a social construct that is maintained through time by myriad social interactions, exchanges, and negotiations. In reality, however, gender and related behavioral expectations are taken so much for granted that most people are raised to believe that gender is biologically based rather than a social product.

These beliefs about the origins of gender are not insignificant. When we believe that gender is biological, we think that there is no possibility for changing gender behavior. Belief in the biological sources of gender behavior thus accepts a particular kind of biological determinism, and reduces opportunities for modifying problematic patterns of gender behavior. By contrast, belief in the social sources of gender behavior implies quite clearly that there are many possibilities for changing gender patterns. When our starting point is the fact that gender behavior is learned, we can work together for much different outcomes.

One of the pernicious consequences of accepting biological explanations about gender differences is that we resist others' attempts to increase gender equity and gender justice. When we base our thinking on the conviction that biology cannot be changed, we close out possibilities for the twenty-first century—at a time when increased gender diversity needs to be accepted rather than rejected.

Making deliberate use of social intelligence is an effective way to become less reactive—as individuals, groups, and societies—to conventional gender designations. It is not enough to identify trends in gender representations, institutional gender arrangements, and patterns of gender behavior throughout history. We also need to be aware of increased gender possibilities for the twenty-first century.

One of the critical aspects of gender issues for the future is the increasing public recognition given to differences in sexual orientations. In order to work toward a truly diverse society, we need to accept many varieties of sexual orientation such as gay, lesbian, bisexual, transgendered, and transvestite sexuality. There are no specific ranges of behavior or expectations for a particular gender that are shared by all men or all women. The gender possibilities among and between men and women are infinite. Although we tend to form collective wholes in order to survive, at the same time we are completely distinctive as individuals with respect to gender, sexual orientation, and other personal or social characteristics.

A twentieth century trend of accepting gender diversity has taken hold in some societies. However, social intelligence suggests that we cannot turn back the clock, and that the twenty-first century must have more public recognition and public acceptance of sexual diversity if we are to survive and thrive. We cannot continue to suppress the strong force of sexuality because everyone's well-being is dependent on not only tolerating but also welcoming this social reality in our everyday routines. Furthermore, none of us benefits in the long run if we resist the presence of recently evolved non-coercive gender arrangements.

Social intelligence suggests that once we accept gender diversity in personal spheres and the workplace, there will be more gender equality throughout society. Historically there has been a grassroots momentum in changing sexual arrangements and gendered social institutions. When men, women, and sexual minorities work together as members of the same team, we survive and thrive more effectively as a society and as an international community.

One of the significant aspects of gender and sexual orientation is the continuing existence of social hierarchies that value different genders and different sexual orientations with basic social honor and respect. White males have historically held high status in these hierarchies, whereas women and minority sexual orientations have been habitually assigned to positions of lower status. In part these social hierarchies reflect a conventional division of labor between men and women, which has deep-seated evolutionary and historical roots.

Biological differences have been used as a justification to perpetuate gender roles and a division of labor with regard to assuming family care and domestic responsibilities. The roles and tasks of maintaining families and households are conventionally associated with women. However, social intelligence confirms that these kinds of family and domestic roles are learned, and that individual interest and social pressures have prevented men as a group from embracing these roles. Although there have always been exceptions to this trend, the overwhelming preponderance of men have been more interested in maintaining the economic and social privileges of their higher status in social hierarchies than in sharing care and labor responsibilities at home.

The twentieth century showed some increases in men's family involvement. However, these shifts are not as marked as might have been expected, given the number of different factual reports that have been assembled, as well as the issues of equity that have been articulated and supported by feminists. Social intelligence suggests that the twenty-first century must show more progress in reducing these kinds of gender inequities if we are to create a more just and balanced society. These changes are necessary because only then will we have more possibilities for survival and fulfillment as a society and as an international community.

Religion

The twenty-first century will have to understand similarities and contrasts in different kinds of belief systems. Although secular belief systems, such as political ideologies, have much in common with religions, secular beliefs do not bring with them the same kind of sanctions and sacred rituals as religious beliefs. Secular belief systems have their own kinds of beliefs and rituals, but they are less oriented to other-worldliness, and less able to wield a continuing influence over routine perceptions and everyday experiences.

Although some predictions have been made that religion will become obsolete in the future, largely due to the ever-increasing importance and sophistication of scientific explanations of the universe, social intelligence suggests that religion and other kinds of belief systems are here to stay. The historical record shows that people in widely differing cultures and societies need to have congruent beliefs about the nature of their existence in order to find meaning in harsh conditions, crises, and everyday behavior.

In spite of these kinds of continuities in religions, religions in the twenty-first century may appear in different forms and serve different purposes. Traditional orthodoxies, although they bring security through their long-established beliefs and practices, such as reassuring believers about life after death, may be less able to move with the times than more flexible belief systems. In the final analysis, social intelligence shows us that religions have to accommodate and adapt to their particular social settings if they are to be able to truly support their believers.

Another concern is that religions often engender conflict among themselves, even if there is no direct manipulation of beliefs held by their followers. This means that societies of the twenty-first century need to develop strategies that will reduce conflict among religions, such as increasing the possibilities for meaningful interfaith dialogues. In many respects, we have more of a need to understand each other through familiarizing ourselves with religions we do not know, than to continue to refine our own beliefs within a particular religion. These are tasks that must be done because if we leave relationships among religions as they are, there will continue to be friction and conflict among religious beliefs that cannot be reconciled easily.

To the extent that people in different countries need to participate in envisioning possibilities for the twenty-first century, common denominators among religions will have to be found and used as a foundation for international exchanges. In some respects, different religions can be used as a source for constructing a global ethic that could guide actions taken on behalf of international human rights. If we are to live as a global community, we have to establish standards for governing behavior that originate in contrasting cultural settings.

Another way to increase harmony among different religions is to concentrate more on similarities in spiritual beliefs than on differences in religious community rituals. All religions have their own cultures, but it is the essence of religious values that inspires believers and non-believers alike. Social intelligence suggests that, in some respects, many religions move in similar directions, so that being a devoted believer in one religion has meaningful similarities with another devoted believer of another religion.

Historically, men have officiated in more religions than women. The needs of the twenty-first century call for more balance between men and women within religious hierarchies, and a lessening of hierarchical relations within and among religions. Because many religions concern themselves with social justice, all kinds of hypocrisy within religions need to be decreased as soon as possible. The twenty-first century cannot be a century of enlightenment if religions do not practice what they preach.

XII. Social Intelligence and the Twenty-First Century

Another important focus for religions in the twenty-first century should be to deliberately increase tolerance and respect for each other. Religious beliefs are frequently intense, with a heightened sense of moral rectitude. However, relationships among religions cannot be constructive and creative unless there is a genuine appreciation for each other's particular strengths, values, and contributions. A true community of believers has to have a meaningful and effective outreach to other communities, so that parochial insularity is minimized. Survival and fulfillment in the twenty-first century depend on articulating some important shared values, sharing a breadth of vision, and cultivating deep understanding. Respecting different religions is one way to achieve this goal.

Class

An additional dimension of social intelligence that is critically needed in our approaches to problems and situations in the twenty-first century is our awareness of and knowledge about different kinds of social classes and their relationships to each other. We must consider how we share or do not share social class experiences, if we are to understand and change class relations in our interpersonal exchanges and in broad social dynamics in the twenty-first century. For example, it is easier to have a sense of belonging with others when we realize that our daily situations and life chances are similar to theirs. Because of this, members of the same gender, race, ethnic group, or sexual orientation can see more clearly how they are defined and labeled by others. They can also understand how different kinds of treatment and thinking establish or even institutionalize patterns of expectations, prejudice, and discrimination throughout society in the twenty-first century.

Understanding the continuing significance of social classes in the twenty-first century necessarily draws upon historical aspects of some of these shared experiences. By examining trends in class differences over long periods of time, we can more easily see how inequities in today's societies have longstanding continuities and traditions. For example, some groups or social classes have been kept in lower statuses largely to benefit those who have higher statuses. When social intelligence enables us to see these kinds of social class exchanges as historical trends, we add depth to our understanding of the importance of social classes in our limited lifetimes and in the twenty-first century. SI also alerts us to the difficulties and resistance we will inevitably encounter as we try to make changes with regard to these aspects of society and the international community in the present and in the future.

When we understand the complexities of our own social class affiliations more fully, we are in a better position to assess the differences and stark contrasts in the social conditions that are perpetuated among social classes. We are also more able to use social intelligence about these class differences to decrease them. When we plan changes for the twenty-first century, we realize that more effective and durable social changes can occur when people take their class differences into account, and we can even use social classes as a starting point for dealing with major social issues such as human rights.

However, even when we use social intelligence to reduce class differences, we may not realistically be able to achieve conditions that even approximate just or egalitarian social relations. Nevertheless, using SI will help us to begin to tackle problems of social inequality in the twenty-first century, especially when members of at least one social class experience relative deprivation as a characteristic or a consequence of their own class memberships. Social intelligence helps us to understand that prejudice and discrimination are not individual, unique phenomena, but rather are damaging and destructive patterns of behavior that limit the opportunities and life chances of particular groups and classes in society in the present and, unless checked, in the future.

When members of the younger generation are raised to understand what class differences are and what they mean for insiders and outsiders, as well as to see the social injustices that evolve from these same class differences, there is a greater likelihood that social inequalities and other injustices will be rectified through future actions and strategies. In principle, class differences need to be minimized, or at least reduced, in order to create a stronger sense of belonging to societies and to the international community. This is not to say that everyone should become more alike, but rather that all individual and group differences need to be valued and appreciated for their particular contributions to the whole, rather than exploited, if we are to survive and thrive in the twenty-first century.

XII. Social Intelligence and the Twenty-First Century

Social intelligence about social classes awakens us to the social reality of the continuing power and influence of conflicts of interest in society at large. However, even given this precarious social reality, societies and the global community in the twenty-first century are more likely to survive and thrive when we use SI to prevent class differences from dividing populations and creating schisms that lead to intense conflict or war. Although we cannot hope to be in harmony with others at all times, a substantial degree of tolerance and respect is needed in order for society and the global community to continue to exist, especially in times of rapid change.

Culture

Because we are social and therefore cultural beings, it is impossible for us not to be concerned about future trends in culture, and their impact on the twenty-first century. However, given the reality of the inevitability of cultural transmission, social intelligence offers us more thoughtful and more deliberate ways to be in the twenty-first century. When we use it to think more deeply and clearly about the content of our cultural messages to members of the younger generation, we can act in ways that will avoid some of the negative consequences that occur when we automatically communicate negative beliefs, values, and ideals.

Culture is an amalgam of at times contradictory values, beliefs, and ideals that have already served to help individuals and societies to adapt to different types of social change. New values, beliefs, and ideals can also initiate and create social changes, such as the social movements of human rights or women's rights, so that consequently different social adaptations are made. In these respects, and even in the most commonplace everyday situations that appear to be static and unrelated to social change, culture is an extremely pervasive and significant resource for the twenty-first century. At all times, we routinely draw upon culture to make sense of our lives, our social situations, the world at large, our purposes, and our directions. For example, we can only dream in cultural terms, and we are compelled to use cultural symbols whenever we interact with others.

When we make deliberate use of social intelligence to guide us in how to build more constructive cultures, we are forced to become more selective about what aspects of culture we want to survive for the twenty-first century. Our willingness to choose values, beliefs, and ideals that we think will make the greatest difference in the lives of others and in the future compels us to act more responsibly in our cultural communications. Although it would not be socially intelligent to force our beliefs on others, SI is a reliable means whereby we can become stronger examples of what we want culture to be in the twenty-first century when we interact on a daily basis. No one can coerce us to accept the values of society's status quo as right or just. Social intelligence shows us that we have the freedom to make our own declarations of independence and expressions of social justice in whatever we say, and more importantly in how we behave.

The very act of transmitting our beliefs, especially to members of the next generation, strengthens them and our commitment to these same beliefs and values for the twenty-first century. We gain in integrity and social influence from passing on values we believe in to others. Even though knowledge itself, such as social intelligence, is a useful means to convince others of the importance of aiming for social justice, in the long run we are all challenged to take a stand for our highest values and ideals. In reality, however, we are often not up to doing what it takes to accept this challenge. Because of the problems and difficulties involved in taking a stand for our beliefs and values, we usually choose to compromise by not making an optimal cultural communication. Unfortunately, although this resolution of the dilemma may not seem like too much of an opportunity missed, in the long run such a lack of courage will bring negative consequences in its wake for ourselves, for the next generation, and for the future of civilization.

On a more positive level the gifts we receive, when we dedicate ourselves to passing culture on in socially intelligent ways, are indescribable and immeasurable. Because of the depth of our lived experiences and our own social intelligence, we have a capacity that will make the world a better place in dependable ways. Our social and moral senses, which we derive from significant others, are at our disposal to increase the power of good in the world. Thus, although we may not gain worldly recognition or material benefits by doing so, passing culture on in socially intelligent ways can be a direct means to build civilization rather than tear it down, as well as a means to be truly constructive in all we do. When we use our social intelligence to deliberately create a firm foundation for the cultures of the twenty-first century, we essentially rise to the challenge of doing a higher good. This effort also helps us to lead the world to a better place, so that more people can benefit from, and glory in, life itself.

Society

Using social intelligence to understand how we are related to society and to the international community is an important aspect of our preparedness for the twenty-first century. Once we see and recognize the influence and significance of social interdependence in our lives, we are in a sufficiently strong position to be able to plan for the future, and especially to tackle problems of the twenty-first century. The actions involved in passing SI on to others will also deepen our own appreciation of the many complex social and global dimensions of our everyday behavior.

We bring society into our views of the world in the twenty-first century by studying about our own and other countries, or by traveling abroad in order to actually experience different ways of doing things. When we undertake such travels, we create many opportunities to practice and increase our social intelligence. Because we learn most from doing, deliberately exposing ourselves to different societies deepens our understanding and empathy for others. Thus we participate in the best of all worlds when we become less ethnocentric and parochial.

Studying history and evolution prepares us for the twenty-first century because we see how important it is to consider society as a whole, as well as the international community and Planet Earth, in formulating specific plans and strategies for intervention. Whatever context we situate ourselves in through our thoughts and actions, our social intelligence directs us to a broad view of our everyday lives that may not be apparent in our day-to-day interactions. Seeing ourselves on a wide screen enables us to be more human, as well as to be more deliberate and accurate in formulating our goals for action.

A focus on society highlights the ways in which complex networks of relationships, power, and influence have an impact on the quality of our daily existence. There is no way that we can go about our daily work in isolation from others, or without having to pay attention to the presence and needs of others. Reciprocity and interaction continue to be the name of the game in being a member of society and the world community in the twenty-first century. On both small and large scales of survival and fulfillment, we are citizens of society and the world in the past, present, and future.

So if we are to come full circle and ask how social intelligence can help us to face and deal with the twenty-first century, we must take great care to include these broad perspectives in our assessments. We cannot be socially intelligent without situating ourselves in society and in the world, and we cannot be enlightened about our everyday behavior unless we are socially intelligent. Planning for the twenty-first century must include asking the biggest and most basic questions about survival and fulfillment within these contexts. Our visions about society and the world will help us to assess our priorities, and therefore make it more likely that we accomplish the goals and interventions that we design.

In order to understand the continuing impact of society on what we do, we need to see the relationships among family, gender, religion, class, and culture within societies. When we appreciate the systemic dependencies among these different social influences, we are more likely to be able to identify the networks in relationships among all societies and within the international community. This capacity to think in terms of interdependent social systems is a strong and vital component of social intelligence, which helps us to understand and act in the twenty-first century.

If the future decades are to mark progress in history, we need to use our social intelligence. Understanding what society means to us is a crucial aspect of our readiness to increase social justice in the twenty-first century. In fact, we cannot be sure we will make wise decisions about the future unless we use the resources of SI in our negotiations and exchanges. It is a silver bullet for our continued successes, and for fighting the many social problems and challenges that persist in today's society.

The usefulness of the broad perspective of society is based on the principle that the whole of any particular society, or of the international community, is more powerful than the sum of its individual parts. We are beholden to society's well being in such a way that any denial or minimization of the importance of this relatedness has dire consequences. Social intelligence helps us to honor the interdependent nature of our humanness, and to continue to build a civilized world in the twenty-first century. The shared need to do this is one of our primary obligations to the next generations and the worlds to come.

Suggested Reading

Bartky, Sandra. 1990. *Femininity and Domination*. New York: Routledge.

Benedict, Ruth. 1934. *Patterns of Culture*. Boston and New York: Houghton Mifflin.

Berger, Peter L. 1963. *Invitation to Sociology: A Humanistic Perspective*. Garden City, NY: Doubleday.

Berger, Peter L., and Thomas Luckmann. 1966. *The Social Construction of Reality*. Garden City, NY: Doubleday.

Bernard, Jessie. 1987. *The Female World from a Global Perspective*. Bloomington, IN: Indiana University Press.

Berrick, Jill Duerr. 1995. *Faces of Poverty: Portraits of Women and Children on Welfare*. New York: Oxford University Press.

Bottomore, T. B. 1966. *Classes in Modern Society*. New York: Pantheon Books.

Chafetz, Janet Saltzman. 1990. *Gender Equity: An Integrated Theory of Stability and Change*. Newbury Park, CA: Sage Publications.

Charon, Joel M. 1999. *The Meaning of Sociology*. Upper Saddle River, NJ: Prentice Hall.

Charon, Joel M. 2001. *Ten Questions: A Sociological Perspective*. Belmont, CA: Wadsworth.

Collins, Randall. 1979. *The Credential Society: An Historical Sociology of Education and Stratification*. New York: Academic Press.

Crompton, Rosemary. 1993. *Class and Stratification: An Introduction to Current Debates*. Cambridge, MA: Polity Press.

Epstein, Cynthia Fuchs. 1988. *Deceptive Distinctions: Sex, Gender, and the Social Order*. New Haven, CT: Yale University Press.

Gilligan, Carol. 1982. *In a Different Voice*. Cambridge, MA: Harvard University Press.

Goffman, Erving. 1959. *The Presentation of Self in Everyday Life*. Garden City, NY: Doubleday.

Lorber, Judith. 1993. *Paradoxes of Gender*. New Haven, CT: Yale University Press.

Mills, C. Wright. 1956. *The Power Elite*. New York: Oxford University Press.

Mills, C. Wright. 1959. *The Sociological Imagination*. New York: Oxford University Press.

Riesman, David. 1961. *The Lonely Crowd: A Study of the Changing American Character*. New Haven, CT: Yale University Press.

Skolnick, Arlene, and Jerome Skolnick. 1997. *Family in Transition*. New York: Addison-Wesley.

Smedley, Audrey. 1993. *Race in North America: Origin and Evolution of a Worldview*. Boulder, CO: Westview.

Tumin, Melvin M. 1985. *Social Stratification: The Forms and Functions of Inequality*. Englewood Cliffs, NJ: Prentice-Hall.

Wilson, Bryan. 1982. *Religion in Sociological Perspective*. New York: Oxford University Press.

Suggested Reading

Wilson, William J. 1973. *Power, Racism, and Privilege.* New York: Macmillan.

Wilson, William J. 1987. *The Truly Disadvantaged: The Inner City, the Underclass, and Public Policy.* Chicago: University of Chicago Press.

With many thanks to my colleagues at Georgetown University Sociology and Anthropology Department, The Bowen Center for the Study of the Family, Sociological Practice Association, and Society for Applied Sociology. I am also greatly indebted to my clients and students, who have taught me so much, and to my wonderful American and English families, who continue to put up with me on a daily basis.